THE ILLUMINATION CODEX
GATEWAY TWO PART TWO

COSMIC CHRIST TRANSMISSIONS

THE MINISTRY OF LIGHT

MICHAEL GARBER

MICHAEL GARBER

Printed in the United States of America
First Printing 2021
First Edition 2021

Second Edition

ISBNs:
Softcover 978-1-959561-07-1
eBook 978-1-959561-08-8

10 9 8 7 6 5 4 3 2 1

The
Illumination
Codex

Table of Contents

ACKNOWLEDGMENTS

I bow in humble recognition of the One Light of Consciousness, the Source of my being and the source of all knowledge and wisdom. I give gratitude to the Supreme for dreaming me into existence and allowing me to have the conscious experience of life and the crafting of this codex.

I bow in love and gratitude to my dear beloved partner Ron Amit, a true gift of the Divine, for all the many ways he supports me in my life. I am blessed beyond measure to have such a brilliant master of love, compassion, and divine service to walk this earthly life with. Thank you for all that you do, seen and unseen, to amplify joy and higher consciousness for me and all beings in the Cosmos. I love you across all space, time, and dimensions.

I send gratitude to my friends and clients who have brought forth the lost stories of Creation through their Illuminated Quantum Healing hypnosis sessions. Thank you for being the powerful Light beacons that you are!

I send deep gratitude to my many modern scribes who assisted me in the transcription work. Thank you for helping me capture these incredible client stories so that the world can remember our cosmic divine heritage.

Bless all the beings, seen and unseen, who have helped me craft this material so that you, the reader, can be nourished on your path of Ascension. May you, the reader, be blessed infinitely and discover the highest truth of your being. May ascended consciousness, liberation, and divine unification be yours in this very life!

DEDICATION AND INVOCATION

This book is dedicated to the infinite expressions of our Oneself, for the celebration of our many incarnations, past, present, and future, and the lessons we have learned throughout eternity. May these words and the energy they carry be a potent force for awakening for all seekers of Unconditional Love and divine Truth. May this transmission support the reactivation and restoration of humanity's divine blueprint upon planet Earth and accelerate the realization of our eternal unity and oneness with all of Creation.

Let us join in prayer, honoring and sending gratitude to the Supreme Intelligent Source of Creation, the omniscient, omnipotent, omnipresent, transcendental Divine Source that is our True Nature.

Let us honor and send gratitude to the higher Light realms and the beings of Light who guide and protect Creation's evolution. Let us honor and send gratitude to our star lineages and those who support us from beyond the Earth. Let us receive your love and blessings now as we remember our cosmic ancestry and our role in the higher evolutionary plan for Creation.

Let us honor and send gratitude to our Earth Mother and her many dimensions and manifestations of Life including the animal, plant, bacterial, fungal, protozoan, mineral, crystalline, and elemental beings who contribute to her dynamic, regenerative biomes. These writings are offered as salve and balm to heal and bless our beloved Gaia, our Earth Mother and Divine Sister. May her waters be pure, her soil rich, her air clean, and may all beings, seen and unseen, within her living biofield know lasting peace forever and ever.

Let us honor and send gratitude to the wisdom and guidance from the seven directions of East, South, West, North, Above, Below, and Within. Let us call back our soul fragments scattered through time and space so that we may anchor ourselves HERE and NOW in this eternal moment of infinite potential to witness the unfolding manifestation of the Divine Plan.

Let us honor and send gratitude to the elements of Earth, Air, Fire, Water, and Ether that create the foundation of our evolutionary experience in form. May the Light of Consciousness awaken swiftly in each of us as we remember our True Nature beyond names and forms.

Let us honor and send gratitude to our ancestors and the many souls who have shared their light upon the Earth. Let us send special thanks to those who dedicated their lives to passing on the Mysteries and sacred knowledge of the Divine so that we may NOW stand at this Grand Turning of the Ages, with the support of all who have come and all who are destined to live upon this great Earth.

I call forth the full remembering of our divinity and the weaving of a new story of harmony and peace for all of Life upon the Earth. May we shed our stories of limitation and suffering and step forward into a new era as People of Light, cosmic co-citizens, and ambassadors for the Living Light of Creation.

Hallelujah! Jai! Aho! Blessed Be! Amen! And so, it is! Om!

GUIDANCE FOR READING THIS BOOK

The Illumination Codex is a multidimensional library for the path of Ascension. It is holographic by nature as each chapter contains a multitude of keycodes to activate ancient cellular memory and trigger multidimensional awareness and higher consciousness integration. As you read the material, your Inner Being will offer flashes of insight and higher perception into your awareness to assist you in healing, spiritual activation, and cosmic remembrance. I recommend using a highlighter, journaling your process, and using other resources to research and enhance your understanding of the topics presented in this book.

A major influence for this material comes from my work as a past-life regression hypnotherapist using the methods we have codified into a technique called Illuminated Quantum Healing (IQH). While in a deep hypnotic trance, my clients experience other lifetimes and other planetary civilizations and communicate with advanced intelligent species from beyond the Earth and Earth plane. The information contained in this book is a summary of my understanding of all that I have learned through my clients as they journeyed to the ancient past, probable timelines of the future, and higher planes of Light. There are many transcriptions of IQH sessions included in the book for you to have your own unique interpretation and multidimensional experience with the material.

This book contains a diverse collection of spiritual information from a variety of wisdom traditions that I have studied in my life. These writings are my own interpretations and understandings of these different concepts that have helped me in my awakening journey and do not necessarily speak for the lineages themselves. This presentation of information is meant as a collection of keys to unlock the wisdom that is already encoded within you. None of it is meant to become dogmatic as consciousness revelation and ascendency will open us continuously to higher and higher truths and understanding.

I confess that I share this transmission as a fellow traveler on the path of awakening. I have my own limitations, my own egoic nature, and my own struggles. I am capable of error and ignorance just as any other person. This presentation of information is what I have found along my path which has triggered awakening and helped me on my path back home to my Self. My prayer is that this book will become deeply meaningful for you and be a guiding light back to your own liberated being.

While reading this material, you may come across something in the text that triggers something within you that is uncomfortable. Maybe it is words that I use, perspectives that I share, or something else that may bring up resistance, judgment, anger, guilt, and so on. This is a wonderful opportunity to investigate the origin of the reactive mental and emotional patterns that create such experiences. The origin may come from earlier stages of your life or previous lifetimes. Use this as an opportunity to reconcile those parts of your consciousness through spiritual inquiry and self-study so that you may realize deeper states of wholeness and clarity.

This text is intended to activate 'gnosis,' a direct experience and knowledge of the divine presence within and around you. I do not recommend blind faith in any concept or religious doctrine. The information in this book is not meant to be treated as religious dogma that cannot be questioned or developed further. It is meant to be utilized to unlock the truth that lives within your very being. I am not writing this intending to change people's beliefs or convert anyone. I am simply relaying the summary of my life's research on the quest for spiritual truth. If something from the material does not resonate as truth in your heart, release it and move on to the next part of the transmission. Use the philosophy and information in this text to stimulate your expansion and the embodiment of YOUR deepest truth and to strengthen your relationship and innate connection with the Divine.

Another thing to mention is capitalization. You will notice that there are words that are not normally capitalized in other books and sacred texts that are capitalized in this text. My intention behind this was to add spiritual dimensionality to words that describe qualities or names of the Divine.

Typically, when I speak of light in this book, I am speaking about higher-dimensional, intelligently-encoded subtle energy and not conventional light from a light bulb. When I speak about "energy," I am speaking about subtle energy which exists beyond the visible light spectrum for most people. Many are becoming sensitive to subtle energy (i.e., multisensory, intuitive, psychic) and are developing the ability to sense and perceive this energy through extrasensory perception. All of humanity is evolving towards being able to perceive and interact with subtle energy and higher cosmic intelligence and consciousness.

The use of the term consciousness fluctuates throughout the book and can mean different things. When I speak of pure Consciousness I am speaking about your True Self as Source Consciousness, the Absolute, the Eternal Witness of all Creation, pure Awareness and Existence itself. Other times I will speak of consciousness as in variations of the mind such as unity consciousness or separation consciousness. All forms of consciousness, all experiences of the mind, borrow existence from the One Light of Consciousness and you are that!

I tried my best to organize this text in a way that can be read from front to back like any regular book, but it can also be read any way you feel intuitively called to read it. Part of the reason for the size of this codex is because it is difficult to explain one part without understanding many other components. In my effort to answer all potential and probable questions about ascension, I wrote everything I could on this multifaceted, multidimensional topic.

As you make your journey through this material, there are three stages to help integrate the information and use it to fuel your awakening to your True Nature:

Stage One: Listening (*Sravana*) As you read or listen to the material in this book, allow it to penetrate deeply and work with your inner philosophical understanding. Listen deeply to your Inner Being for there will be flashes of insight and knowing that emerge within your inner consciousness space.

Stage Two: Reflection (*Manana*) Try your best to understand the information contained in this book through self-inquiry and inner philosophical pondering. I am not asking for you to blindly believe any of this transmission. Think of this information as an active hypothesis. You do not have to believe it, but you can reflect over the information and see how it applies to your life.

Stage Three: Integration/Meditation (*Nididhyasana*) As you take in the words in stage one and convert the words to knowledge and understanding in stage two, you move into conviction and integration of knowledge in stage three as you crystallize and embody the Self-knowledge of "I am Pure Consciousness." As you go about your daily life, use the knowledge you have gained to interrupt habit and conditioned thought and re-direct your mind toward the Light of Consciousness that you are.

Gateways of Entry

Besides reading front-to-back or intuitively hopping around, I have created six gateways for you to enter the presentation of the material. I have created one large book that has all of the Illumination Codex material and separated the material into separately published volumes to make the information more digestible. The Gateways are as follows:

GATEWAY ONE: ASCENSION INITIATION: KEYS FOR HIGHER EVOLUTION gives an overall understanding of Ascension, reincarnation, universal law, and a theoretical and philosophical framework concerning Cosmic Evolution. This is an excellent place to start if you are open and eager to learn about these subjects and awakening, you may want to start in Gateway Three.

GATEWAY TWO: AKASHIC DATABASE contains a wide variety of Illuminated Quantum Healing session transcriptions describing key figures and events in the history of Creation, galactic history, ancient planetary history, and probable future timelines of New Earth from clients in hypnotic visionary states. This is a suitable place to enter the material if you already have a general understanding of multidimensionality, galactic civilizations, and the process of personal and planetary ascension. This gateway is conveniently separated into QUANTUM ORIGINS, COSMIC CHRIST TRANSMISSIONS, and NEW EARTH TRANSMISSIONS. If you find yourself resistant to those ideas and are new to these subjects. I recommend developing a meditation practice parallel to reading this material as the transcripts are deeply activating on multiple levels.

GATEWAY THREE: PATH OF AWAKENING: KEYS FOR TRANSFIGURATION is an in-depth collection of spiritual and philosophical wisdom to support personal, relational, and planetary healing. If you are in the beginning stages of awakening or moving through a deep healing process, you may wish to start here so you can develop your consciousness and prepare your mind and body for higher level initiation into the Mysteries.

GATEWAY FOUR: CHAKRA YOGA DISCOURSE transmits deeper

insight into the themes and physio-psycho-spiritual domains of the vortices of life force and perception called the *chakras*. Each section transmits valuable information to understand the common distortions in these processing centers and how to activate and reconcile each center.

GATEWAY FIVE: LAYING HANDS: REIKI & BEYOND is a full manual for learning the art of the laying of hands for healing. The manual clearly describes all the stages, steps, and practices to perform powerfully transformative hands-on-healing sessions for yourself, others, and even in groups. This manual would be acceptable for any Level 1 and Level 2 Reiki course.

GATEWAY SIX: ASCENSION LEXICON is a glossary of commonly used words to describe the process of awakening and ascension. These definitions act as keycode activators to unlock deeper meaning and inner wisdom. Many words used in spiritual/ascension circles are convoluted and sometimes lose their impact because they are misused or misunderstood. I may use words in a way you are not familiar with, or I may use words differently than you. I tried my best to make a glossary with foundational vocabulary to assist with understanding the material. You may wish to read the ASCENSION LEXICON before journeying through the main text of the book.

Bless you on your personal path through this material. May the light in your heart guide you with ease and grace on your journey of initiation with *The Illumination Codex*.

Awakening to the Quantum Reality

In the Summer of 2016, I was given a book that forever changed my life's direction called *The Three Waves of Volunteers and the New Earth* by Dolores Cannon. This book was a huge catalyst in my spiritual awakening. Reading the text stirred something deep within me and resonated profoundly with my heart's truth. The book's pages sent waves of energy down my spine as I began to awaken to a higher consciousness reality and remember my purpose for being born upon the Earth at this time.

Dolores Cannon was a world-renowned hypnotherapist specializing in past-life regression. To understand the power of regressive hypnosis, we also need to understand the workings of the mind. The mind can be separated into three categories: the conscious mind, the subconscious mind, and the superconscious mind.

The conscious mind is the ego/personality part of the mind. This active part of the mind uses limited information from the environment and past experiences to make decisions and take care of the body.

The subconscious mind is the recording device of our mind. It records incredible amounts of information at every moment. We easily pull data from the subconscious when we think about something from our past as we access memory.

Deeper in the subconscious, sometimes called the unconscious mind, we have unconscious memories and information, including societal conditioning, painful traumas from this life that are too painful to remember, and memories from other lifetimes. Even though this information is not in the conscious mind, it silently influences our day-to-day experience as reactive emotional momentum, called *samskaras* in Sanskrit, from past events which overlay and filter our experience of the present moment. These subconscious patterns are like applications running in the background of smartphones that quietly drain the processing speed and battery, silently influencing processor speed and functionality.

The superconscious mind is a higher mind capacity that gives us access to intuitive information, extrasensory perception, non-local consciousness, creative genius, universal connection, and access to divine consciousness. This part of the mind is mostly undiscovered and underdeveloped in most of humanity.

Dolores created a unique method of hypnosis, Quantum Healing Hypnosis Technique (QHHT), that opened a doorway to the client's subconscious mind to explore other lifetimes and realms in Creation. When I use the word "quantum," I am speaking to the fabric of Consciousness, the multidimensional unified field of Creation. When clients are in these hypnotic states, they tap into the part of their consciousness that is nonlocal and connected to All That Is. This includes access to other lifetimes, other realities and dimensions, and other intelligent consciousness forms (i.e., higher-dimensional light beings, telepathic extraterrestrials, etc.). Through this experience, clients came to understand another perspective and origin of self-sabotaging and limiting beliefs that were playing out in this life and the core mental/emotional patterns that create illness and disease.

During her sessions, Dolores started to contact a part of her clients' consciousness that seemed to have endless knowledge and wisdom. She called this aspect of her clients the Subconscious or the SC. Others have called this the Higher Self, the oversoul, superconsciousness, or the cosmic consciousness. I prefer the term Higher Self and superconscious mind and go into great detail of how to activate and evolve superconsciousness throughout this text. While the information was limitless, the SC/Higher Self would only answer questions in a way that was appropriate for the client's learning path and honored their free will. When working with the SC, both Dolores and the client described powerful healing energy in their bodies and the treatment room. Clients often reported instantaneous healing as they were transformed from the inside out during the session. While this may seem too good to be true, there are countless documented and measurable occurrences where clients received lasting miraculous healing through these types of sessions.

When she would work with the Higher Self, this higher consciousness identity and supportive Light team would speak through the client as a collective consciousness as if the client were speaking in third-person perspective about themselves. "We are always guiding her. We wish she would follow her intuition more." and "We are beginning to use white light to heal this now." are common examples of how "They" (i.e., SC/Higher Self) express themselves and heal the client during the session.

The healing work is always done with unconditional love and honors the free will and sovereignty of the client. If instantaneous healing was not "appropriate" for the client's growth and spiritual maturation, "They" would suggest what steps the client should take to heal themself. Slowly, over many years, Dolores's work expanded as "They" introduced more components to the healing process so that she could evolve her work and teach it to others.

The Three Waves of Volunteers and the New Earth was one of nineteen books written by Dolores Cannon before her transition out of physical life. Each book contains transcriptions of client sessions describing detailed events from other lives while using her Quantum Healing Hypnosis Technique (QHHT).

Awakening to the Starseed Volunteer Mission

After several years of working with clients worldwide, Dolores noticed a pattern of clients describing a massive galactic and higher dimensional mission to raise the vibration of the planet and shift it into a new reality called the New Earth. The book describes how countless numbers of advanced spiritual beings from distant star systems, and even other universes, volunteered to incarnate on the Earth with a mission to raise consciousness on the planet and assist with this grand transition.

The New Earth is a higher frequency Earth reality that exists in a higher dimension than we are in now. Clients describe a large-scale plan initiated by Source Intelligence (God) to reset life on planet Earth back to the original template of a harmonic environment thriving within diversity. Parallel to this, Dolores's work described a shift in human consciousness from a duality-based mindset to a heart-centered, multidimensional consciousness and a less physical body of light.

The First Wave Volunteers were born beginning around 1945 through the 1970s. They were like a stealthy reconnaissance mission. First on the scene. First to patrol and feel out the collective consciousness vibrations. First to introduce the higher consciousness perspectives to the masses. Many had a difficult and lonely time since there were not many other humans in higher, love-based spiritual consciousness on the planet at the time.

The Second Wave Volunteers were born around the late 1970s through

1990s and are channels for higher spiritual energy and divine wisdom. These souls came in with a higher level of intuitive gifts and are often extremely sensitive to energy. Many are hands-on healers, musicians, vocalists, yoga teachers, and so on. They are space-holders who transmit a new frequency out to the field of Earth, bridging the old ways with the new ways and consciousness of New Earth.

The Third Wave Volunteers, the younger generations, are builders and innovative geniuses in science, spirituality, technology, and so on. They are divinely inspired visionaries that will build the New Earth. They are radical lovers and shine bright with crystalline eyes and have achieved high consciousness levels in other lifetimes. Some of these souls have never had a physical incarnation or have come straight from Source as new souls with pure Light and no karma.

I have been told all the children born at this time are part of this Grand Mission. They are pure souls, evolutionary masters, here to build the New Earth. More is written about the Starseed Mission and phenomena later in this book.

As I was reading Dolores's book, I felt I was reading my own story. I felt the truth in her words. Suddenly so many things made sense about my life. I finally had answers to why I felt so different from others in my community and family. I understood why I felt other people's emotions and could tell what people were thinking. It all started to click together. I was so excited to share the book with Ron, my husband and co-founder of New Earth Ascending, who also deeply resonated with the material.

At the same time, we were beginning to work with an Australian musical group as dancers for their "Return of the Bird Tribes" tour for their album by the same name. Something about the term "bird tribes" caught my attention, and I started to research it. I found the book by the same name, written by Ken Carey, in 1988 that describes a prophecy of high spiritual beings returning to the Earth at a time of spiritual renewal.

Many cultures describe times when culture-bringing beings would come from the heavens or from across the waters to bring technology and information to humanity throughout history. Thoth went to the Egyptians, White Buffalo Calf Woman went to the Native Americans, Quetzalcoatl went to the Aztecs, the Seven Sisters of the Pleiades went to the Aboriginal people of Australia, beings from the Sirius A and B binary star system went to the Dogon people of Mali; and many other stories exist in many other cultures. Carey's book described when these beings would come again during a time of spiritual awakening on the planet.

I was receiving information from multiple directions and was going through a massive realignment with my soul's purpose as I became aware of this greater story and mission. Ron and I went to an arts festival in the desert of Nevada called Burning Man. While we were there, a couple excitedly recognized us as "twin flames" and asked us which star system we had come from. "We are from Sirius. Where are you from? Orion? The Pleiades? Sirius?" she asked. The concept of "starseeds" and "twin flames" was new to me, and I did not know what to say. I saw a special sparkle in the couple's eyes and felt that I should do some research to understand more about it.

After some research and some magical synchronicities, Ron convinced me that we should do the QHHT training and certification process. I was super resistant to learning it because of deep religious programming and egoic structures that made me doubtful of the truthfulness of the work. I was familiar with reincarnation but did not necessarily believe in it. Eventually, I gave in to Ron's suggestion and took the QHHT course.

Evolving Beyond QHHT

In the early stages of practicing QHHT, Ron and I were guided to start doing the sessions online to share the technique's power with as many people as we could. This method was not permitted by the organization because Dolores did not believe it to be safe and her organization does not permit it still. Dolores was an elder and this type of technology was new to her, whereas the younger generations are much more comfortable interfacing with video conferencing.

We have been told by the Higher Consciousness that there is nothing to fear, and NOW is the time to spread these healing methods across the world in whatever way is possible. To honor our lineage and teacher, we stopped using the name QHHT and started experimenting with different names as our way of practicing quantum healing evolved beyond our initial training.

Online sessions are just as powerful as in-person sessions and are often more comfortable and affordable for the client. It is completely safe to facilitate sessions remotely, and we have had countless powerful sessions that have been facilitated in this way. Dolores's organization does not allow adaptation of the QHHT technique. Its practitioners need to perform the method exactly how Dolores taught and not add any modifications or outside techniques. While it is important to protect the work's integrity, this rigidity does not permit the work to expand to its full potential. We are in a time of expansion and evolution, and we must always be open to the transformation and progression of all methods we currently use or risk leaving them in the past as everything on the Earth is evolving.

Another topic that caused us to evolve beyond our initial training of QHHT was the organization's strict denial of negative spiritual attachment and what felt like shaming those who believed in this common experience. Ron and I and other quantum healing practitioners discovered that certain psychological, emotional, and physical imbalances were being created by pervasive energies that did not belong to the client's energy field that had somehow become attached to the client. This includes spirit attachments, curses from past lives, and implants from nefarious beings to name a few. QHHT did not provide us with appropriate training to work with these serious complications. If it were found out that a practitioner had adopted these practices and still operated under the name of QHHT, practitioners could be removed from the QHHT directory.

Many practitioners have reported spontaneous visitation from Dolores through clients under hypnosis where she has encouraged practitioners to follow their intuitive guidance and continue to develop the work through experimentation just as she did when she developed QHHT.

We were inspired greatly by other quantum healing practitioners' extraction methods and crafted our own approaches to clearing pervasive energies and spirit attachments. The reality of negative thought-forms, negative extraterrestrial implants, and entity attachment is too big to ignore, considering so many cases are emerging, not to forget the thousands of years of wisdom and extraction practices passed down by Indigenous peoples and various wisdom traditions.

We never assume that someone has an entity just because they suffer, and we do not bring it up in our intake interview. Once the client is deep in a hypnotic trance, we ask the Higher Self if there are entities or attached energies. If the answer is yes, then we ask questions to understand how this occurred and if the client has anything to learn to release negative attachment. From there, the Higher Self can immediately extract the energy and take it back into the Light for healing. It is all extremely safe, insightful, and benefits all who are involved. We have found that, often, the revelation of spirit attachment or implants will not occur unless the practitioner asks and gives permission for a scan specifically for attached energies. Ron and I believe this is because of the honoring of the free will of the entities involved in the experience of attachment.

In my opinion, to continue to deny such experiences is a disservice to the clients who come to us seeking answers and healing. All practices and traditions can become dogmatic if we do not allow the evolution of thought to take us into new frontiers of consciousness. These are evolutionary practices, and we need to be constantly open to shifting our paradigm so that we can offer the best guidance and support with the changing of times.

Once we started offering quantum healing sessions online, clients started coming to Ron and me from all over the world. Not only were the sessions powerfully healing and transformative for the clients, but we were also going through a rapid transformation as we learned about ancient stories and galactic events from the perspective of souls embodied at those times. While Dolores taught that many people had "potato-picking lives," simple lives with simple themes, it seemed that almost every session of mine had to do with the New Earth Mission, powerful events from the ancient past, and future timelines of Earth.

I soon realized that I was getting a theme and timeline in my sessions. The timeline given to me via my clients describes how Creation came into being, ancient galactic history, the seeding of life on Earth, the rise and fall of ancient civilizations, the true teachings of Jesus through the eyes of people that were closest to him, information about the transformation of the human body to a less dense body of Light, and the evolution of the Earth into the higher frequency reality of New Earth. In less than a year, I went from a reincarnation skeptic to believing that anything is possible, and that the multiverse is more incredible than we can even imagine!

Illuminated Quantum Healing

After years of practicing and evolving how we do this work, Ron and I have created our own quantum healing method that incorporates all that we have learned on our path. This includes facilitating sessions online to reach as many people as possible to assist in this Great Awakening.

Our training method acknowledges spirit attachment and teaches our facilitators how to perform negative spirit releasement. We teach yogic psychology, holistic wellness concepts, and energy healing methods to ensure the practitioner has a thorough understanding of human consciousness and how to lead the client through the ascension process using multiple IQH sessions and mentorship programs. We call our method Illuminated Quantum Healing. IQH can be learned in live classes or through our online course offered on our social network Source⊙Energy.

Illuminated Quantum Healing (IQH) is a personal transformation method for multidimensional holistic healing and consciousness development. IQH incorporates energy healing, meditative practices, yogic philosophy, and hypnosis skills to reconcile limiting subconscious patterning and integrate instantaneous multidimensional healing and wisdom from one's Higher Self.

I am deeply honored to be a part of this work. I am so blessed to have an opportunity to work with such incredible people and energies. Each session that I facilitate nourishes me to the core, and I have the sublime opportunity to observe miraculous instantaneous healing and transformation in my clients. After witnessing the infinite potential of quantum healing hypnosis, I firmly believe that we can ascend beyond all states of illness and disease and that we have infinite support to move beyond the shadows of our past and become a new People of Light.

Getting to the New Earth involves a process of spiritual growth and purification. To transition with the Earth, it is required that we raise our vibration to match the accelerating frequency of the Earth as it changes. Mostly, this is about releasing fear and negative karma. I have written this book as a tool to use for your spiritual awakening and transformation that many are calling Ascension. This is my gift to humanity to help make the process easier and explain different components to cultivate a deeper understanding of this Grand Shift to New Earth and our newly evolving Lightbody.

Spiritual awakening and ascension are available for ALL people no matter what they have done in their past, current economic status, gender expression, sexuality, religion, etc. There are as many paths to the New Earth as there are humans on the planet. No one religion holds the keys or the way to heaven. The power is within YOU!

To support the global ascension process, we have created New Earth Ascending. New Earth Ascending is a non-profit, faith-based organization focused on global ascension and establishing heart-centered, sustainable communities and educational centers around the world.

Alongside Illuminated Quantum Healing (IQH), Ron and I have created other pathways of support for the global ascension process:

1. Embodied Light Reiki Training and Certification
2. New Earth Ascending has three levels of Reiki certification to train people how to channel divine light for healing. These trainings honor the lineage and teachings of the Usui System of Natural Healing while also infusing evolutionary concepts and practices that go beyond standard Reiki training.
3. Online courses for awakening and ascension are available on our private social network Source⊙Energy. The courses include philosophical exploration on several models of spiritual growth and alchemical practices to support your healing, awakening, and ascension. These courses include meditations, holistic wellness education, breathwork, lightbody activation and more. These courses lay foundational understanding for beginners and move through a progression of intermediate and advanced practices and knowledge.
4. TransformOtion was created to support the embodiment of one's Higher Self using dance, somatic movement, yogic practices, meditation, imagination, and energy healing. This fusion of practices helps to purify and repair the physical, etheric, and mental bodies so that one can move beyond perceived limitations into boundless rhythm and flow. Through this interweaving of multiple disciplinary paths, we integrate physicality with transcendental ecstatic play while cultivating a deep connection with and trust in the body's wisdom.

   These ideas and concepts can be used for personal embodiment and activation or infused into performance art to create powerful alchemical experiences for the performer and the audience. This fusion of high art and spiritual transformation creates a multidimensional experience for all who are within the field of performance energies.

5. Source◉Energy is a social network exclusively for those on the path of ascension to connect and share inspiration as we manifest and build a New Earth. We invite all souls who feel aligned with New Earth to join this network and add your unique energy and love to this community. Source◉Energy serves as a pathway of social interaction and is the home of our online courses and training.

6. Children are our future. Youth inspiration and enrichment programming is in development to assist the spiritual activation and consciousness mastery of the youth. NEA is dedicated to creating harmonic environments and rich educational programs to guide youth to connect with cosmic intelligence and embody their divine nature and mastery as they build the New Earth.

Ron and I have dedicated our lives to supporting this Grand Transition. We stand alongside all of you as humanity awakens to its True Nature and becomes a People of Light in the heavenly reality of New Earth.

New Earth Ascending is dedicated to assisting people to realize their divinity and manifest that truth in every aspect of their life. For more information about New Earth Ascending or to contact Michael, please scan the QR code below for a list of resources and links, or visit *www.newearthascending.org*. Be sure to check out our courses including the Illuminated Quantum Healing practitioner course.

New Earth Ascending is a registered 508 (c)(1)(a) Self-Supported Non-profit Church Ministry with a global outreach. We greatly appreciate your support as we create new systems, communities, and schools for the development of the New Earth civilization. If you would like to make a tax-deductible donation to support our mission, please go to:

https://donorbox.org/donationtonewearthascending

Scan with a smart device camera for more information!

NEW EARTH ASCENDING
VISIONARY CREED

We acknowledge the sovereignty and equality of all levels of Creation and support the liberation of all of Life from cycles of suffering. We believe in the power of divine sovereign creatorship endowed to us by God/Source and dedicate our life to Light and Love in service to All. We believe in conscious participation, empowering everyone to activate awakening in themselves and their community.

We recognize free will and surrender our will and desires to the higher will of the Divine. We believe in divine timing and practice trust, patience, and tolerance as we witness the unfoldment of the perfection of the Divine Plan. We believe in the potency of empowering prayer, meditation, and ritual as tools for communication with the Divine for the culmination of spiritual light and divine wisdom. We believe everyone has a direct connection to the Source and no intermediary is needed. When we come together in fellowship, prayer, and devotion, we amplify the light of each individuals' loving intention through our unified, heart-centered consciousness.

We seek to uplift all groups and communities so that we may celebrate our unity, diversity, and wholeness. New Earth Ascending is non-competitive and embraces an ecumenical relationship with all religions and wisdom traditions. We believe in interfaith and inter-spirituality, acknowledging the teachings of Light, Love, and Wisdom in many traditions, philosophies, and cultures. We believe that no single religion holds the keys to the Kingdom of God and the blessings of redemption are available to all people through their unbreakable innate connection to the Godhead.

We believe in the Law of Oneness and that all of Creation emanates from one Divine Source that has both masculine and feminine principles. As we heal and balance the divine masculine and divine feminine principles within us, we embody the divine androgyny of Source and Nature as a harmonic synthesis of Spirit and Matter.

We believe that humanity and planet Earth are going through a rapid physical and spiritual transformation called by many as The Ascension or The Event. We believe this process to be part of a higher evolutionary divine plan guided by the Source of Creation and legions of beings working for the Light. This evolutionary process is multidimensional and is beyond the standard biological evolution spoken of by modern science.

We believe that we, as humanity, are awakening to our spiritual Self and are becoming a heart-based, unity-focused species with higher, multidimensional awareness, which some call Christ Consciousness, Cosmic Consciousness, or 5D Consciousness. We believe this transformation's power is happening through our divinely designed and curated DNA as the physical body transforms into a less dense body of Light with tremendously expanded multidimensional abilities.

We believe that Planet Earth, the sentient being of Gaia, is going through a similar restoration process and will soon transform into a revitalized higher dimensional planet, which many are calling the New Earth. Earth changes, weather events, crumbling institutional structures, frequency fluctuations, and astrological phenomena are all signs that we are nearing that shift into the next Golden Age, where Heaven and Earth become one and all systems of control and limitation will fall away.

We believe that we are supported by benevolent higher dimensional, subterranean, and extraterrestrial beings that work in harmonic collaboration with the higher evolutionary Divine Plan of Source. We believe that soon humanity will be consciously reunited with these benevolent beings and serve the higher evolutionary plan of the Light and Love of Source as cosmic co-citizens of the Multiverse working as one Family of Light in service to all of Creation.

We understand that the pathway of Self/Source-Realization and Ascension is comprised of self-study, self-practice, self-discipline, and steadfastness. We practice self-care and self-purification to clarify our Light. We acknowledge and value the acceleration of this process when we practice together in groupings of two or more in fellowship and worship.

We strive to grow in awareness and focused attention, practicing mindfulness in all areas of our lives to grow as conscious, heart-centered creators. We choose to focus our life positively with faith and knowing that Life is evolving in perfection following the Divine Plan of the Supreme Source.

We believe in the power of intention. We practice nonviolence and non-harmfulness in intention, thought, and action. We strive to release all forms of judgment and dual thinking. We honor the sacred heart's radiant potential and believe loving compassion and understanding to be The Way. We practice the heart-centered qualities of gentleness, reverence, loving-kindness, and forgiveness as pathways to reconciliation to emulate the eternal grace of Source and our Earth Mother, Gaia.

We see that Truth is alive within each of us, and we practice inner reflection to grow in discernment for what energies are resonant with our inner Source and our path. We practice benevolent truthfulness, honesty, straightforwardness, and vulnerability to embody and vocalize our deepest truth.

We value and practice transparency and accountability, believing in the opportunity for spiritual growth through spiritual partnership with our community members. We recognize one another as divine mirrors, reflecting to us where we are in our vibration, beliefs, and intentions.

We practice sacred sexuality as an alchemical tool for Divine Union and Ascension. We strive to purify our intentions and desires to align with Higher Love and authentic connection. We believe in heart-based self and consensual mutual pleasure to unite body, mind, and spirit so that we may deepen in our love and authentic connection to our Divine Self, our partner(s), and Creation.

We practice contentment, acceptance, appreciation, and gratitude for our life's many blessings and lessons. We practice non-attachment, non-possessiveness, non-stealing, non-excess, and sustainability, for all we need is given to us through our alignment with our Creator Source and our connection to our Earth Mother. We practice stewardship and sustainable selfless service, acknowledging our responsibility to take care of the world around us and within.

We practice sacred commerce, investing our resources, time, and energy towards the greater good and sustainability of our community and planet. We believe in reciprocal energy exchange and strive to do so when able. We practice generosity, hospitality, and charitability as reflections of the abundance of the Universe.

We strive to embody and emulate these spiritual principles to manifest the complete liberation of all beings from cycles of suffering and to assist this Grand Transition into the New Earth.

Bless us all!

Gateway Two Part Two: Cosmic Christ Transmissions

The Ministry of Light

ONE

Jesus and the Ministry of Light

One of my spiritual path's driving forces has been the search for the truth of the life of Jesus and the deeper meanings of his ministry. As a young boy, I could not fully believe the version of his life taught to me in church. Something did not sit right with my Inner Being. Jesus taught of unconditional love and the power of a loving God. When I went to certain churches I felt fear, condemnation, and judgment infused into teachings, and the congregations often felt dull and unresponsive. I was not blind to the fact that thousands upon thousands of people had suffered and died because of the Church's actions. I knew in my heart that Jesus's true story had been distorted since his ministry, and I began to search for truth. I knew there had to be more. I prayed and prayed to Jesus and God to show me the Truth.

As a young child, my grandmother taught me that I should not just read about the version of Jesus in the Bible but also develop a relationship with the Living Christ found in my heart. In the darkest of times in my life, I would retreat into my heart in prayer and ask for guidance and support. Without this connection, I would likely be another statistic of someone lost in the shadows of this world. Jesus has been my number one ally in my life. I invite everyone to release the religious dogma teachings and find the powerful love emanations of the Living Christ available in your very own heart.

My willingness to look beyond the approved teachings of the Church led me to Thich Nhat Hahn and his book *Living Buddha, Living Christ*. As many of you know, there is intense fear programming and shaming around reading spiritual books that are not considered "Christian." I read the book secretly, hoping that I would not be digging my way towards an eternity in Hell. Thich Nhat Hahn helped to encourage my maturing soul to find the interconnectedness between the teachings of the Buddha and Christ. I started reading many of Thich Nhat Hahn's books and started to bring my consciousness out of fear and into compassionate mindful awareness.

Much suffering has occurred across this planet over many generations because of the distortion of the story of Jesus's life and his ministry. Much suffering has been created in the name of Christ that was truly service-to-self consciousness seeking power and domination. Christ's core teaching, like Buddhism, is loving compassion.

Some of the most powerful resources I have found beyond my hypnosis sessions have been Dolores Cannon's books of *They Walked with Jesus* and *Jesus and the Essenes*. I have also felt strong resonance and activation with the channeled texts of *Anna: Grandmother of Jesus* by Claire Heartsong and *The Magdalen Manuscript* by Tom Kenyon. I have a deeper trust in hypnosis sessions because the client's conscious mind filter is removed by being in a deep trance. Even then, I still run the new information through my own heart to see if it rings true! Discernment and deep listening are crucial to anyone who is seeking Higher Truth.

Many of my hypnosis sessions included people involved in the Ministry, and their stories reveal a much more compelling story of the life of Jesus than anyone has ever told in any Sunday school lesson. While some may look for differences in the stories to debunk what is untrue, I have found more power in focusing on the themes and storylines from these various sources that are similar and consistent.

Here are some key points from my research into the life of Jesus that can inspire your path and offer healing.

Redemption Plan

Yeshua ben Joseph's life served as a culmination point in the Redemption Plan that has been initiated by many star nations and the Hierarchy of Light for thousands of years. Before his ministry, ascension teachings were only shared with and known by initiates in secret orders and mystery schools. He came to demonstrate the power of christ consciousness and the Truth of Eternal Life publicly. His body and life provided the redemptive vehicle for the reseeding of the Fourth Density coding for humanity and the Earth.

He foretold the changing of our physical bodies into Light bodies and the many changes that would come to the Earth during a Grand Shift, including the return of the Hierarchies of Light and our Star Nation relatives. Here we stand at this grand culmination point, and each of us has been invited to awaken to our divinity and hold the Light of the divine through this grand passageway.

The Prophecy of the Messiah

High initiates in various traditions shared the same prophecy of the coming of a Messiah, a divine being who would come to set humanity free from slavery. While many hoped that this savior was coming to overturn governments and control systems, he was truly coming to overturn the hearts and minds of those who were ready to free themselves from their suffering and karma.

The slavery mindset is the consciousness of humanity in the third dimension. Jesus came to be a wayshower of consciousness — to liberate the everyday person from slave mentality by sharing wisdom held by high initiates for centuries. It is said repeatedly in sessions that Jesus did not want to be worshipped. He certainly did not intend to be the head of a dead religion where people's consciousness and light are limited and controlled. His teaching was of ONENESS, not of hierarchy. While he played a massive role in the Redemption Plan, his life was meant to be a source of inspiration and a model for what a human can embody in a fully awakened consciousness. His life was not meant to be used to confirm our powerlessness or label us as "lower than" and eternally stained. He said, "You will do these things and more." because we ALL can ascend in our consciousness to achieve christ consciousness and claim our own Sonship/Daughtership as Children of God.

The Essenes

The Essene community on Mount Carmel (Nazareth) and Qumran (Dead Sea) were spiritual communities of initiates that lived in close relationship to Source and the Earth. Members of this community studied the secret mysteries of Creation. They were taught advanced meditation and psychic development from childhood. Children were taught how to materialize and move energy with their minds. Each young student was guided into their power and initiated into the sacred arts they were most proficient at. This included hands-on healing, astrology, astral projection, sacred geometry, telepathy, telekinesis, and even telepathic weather modification was taught to the young masters if it was appropriate for their soul's path.

The Essenes shared sacred scrolls and spiritual techniques with a wide net of mystery schools worldwide, including schools of thought from Egypt, the UK, Tibet, India, and more. Once a young student passed all the initiations and education in their home school, the students often traveled to other communities around the world to advance their studies.

Beyond Earthly resources, the Essene's high initiates were communicating with astral beings and benevolent star beings. These ascended beings would share knowledge and wisdom with elect initiates to be shared amongst the community. Many beings from many star systems would incarnate as Essenes to learn and protect the hidden arts of Ascension.

Yeshua ben Joseph and his family were members of the Essene community. From a young age, Yeshua was taught the Mysteries and advanced spiritual practices. He surpassed all the initiations and all the major schools at the time. There are stories in different cultures about his visitations, particularly in India, Tibet, Egypt, and the UK.

Essene Women

Women of the Essene community were equal to men on all levels of their society. They had full authority over their own life and were able to study, own a home, and even divorce if they chose to. This was quite different from the traditional values and perspectives practiced by the local Jewish people of the time.

Mother Mary

Mother Mary, a High Priestess of the Ancient Egyptian Mystery Schools and Mt. Carmel Essene, embodied the Goddess, the Divine Mother, and gave birth to a child conceived by the Light. A select group of high initiates in at least Egypt and Mt. Carmel knew about her soul purpose before the child was conceived. When clients have seen Mother Mary, they describe the Holy Mother with the presence of a cosmic queen, a powerful priestess, and a central force in Ancient Egyptian priestess training. She was a Master of

Light and Consciousness. She was a cosmic conduit channeling powerful energy from distant star systems like the Pleiades into the Earth to activate awakening across the planet. Part of her mastery included the high sacred art of Light Conception.

Joseph, Mother Mary's husband, was a simple man. He worked to provide for his family but was not directly involved in the miraculous world that his son and wife were. He gave Jesus the core teachings a child would need to grow into maturity. They would work together in Joseph's carpentry shop and had a deep love for one another. When Jesus was old enough, Joseph humbly took him to study with the other initiates knowing that his precious young son was destined for great things!

Light Conception

The ancient Egyptian story of Osiris, Isis, and Horus has described the sacred ritual of Light Conception long before the birth of Jesus. After the resurrection of Osiris, Isis conceived her child Horus from the Light Seed of Osiris through a sacred ritual. Through accessing the Higher Planes, the initiates of Isis were taught how to bring a soul into their womb with or without the seed of a man.

Mother Mary learned this ancient ritual to conceive the soul of Yeshua directly from the Divine. Her unwavering faith and crystalline body temple, fortified through arduous spiritual activation, made her the perfect vessel to bring forth the powerful Light force of Yeshua.

The Birth of the Messiah:
Star of Bethlehem

The birth of Yeshua was of extreme importance for the unfolding of the Divine and Galactic Redemption Plan. A rare celestial alignment created a "tear" in the 3D matrix creating an interdimensional pathway for advanced souls to enter the Earth Matrix. In my sessions, clients describe the Star of Bethlehem lightcraft/spaceship with many high beings from throughout the galaxy and higher light dimensions on board. When clients describe the birth scene, they describe powerful love vibrations emanating from the Christ Child. Even the animals in attendance played a part in creating a pristine energetic container for the arrival of Yeshua's soul. Soon after he was born, Yeshua was taken to live in a spiritual community in Egypt to protect his emerging consciousness from the conditioning of the world and to activate his spiritual gifts through training.

Yeshua grew up with the Essenes and in the temples of Egypt between the approximate ages of eight to sixteen. In his childhood, he was surrounded by initiates in constant prayer and spiritual study. Many around him knew what his soul purpose was, and many galactic beings incarnated to support his grand mission. They created a pristine high-frequency environment to protect his mind from being indoctrinated by human conditioning to keep him pure and strong for what was to come. One client described his laughter as a child filling the entire space as if the whole world could feel his innocent child nature. He spent a lot of time in silence, meditation, and spiritual development to maintain his connection to the other realms. A deep understanding of Creation was inherently encoded in his Inner Being and genetics. He wasn't necessarily "taught" but nourished so that he could embody the oversoul mastery he came in with. This high level of spiritual practice helped him maintain his divine alignment so he could be the powerful Light force he was destined to be.

Transcript: Yeshua Begins His Ministry

Around the age of sixteen, Yeshua left Egypt to begin to spread The Word and to start teaching the collective. Here is a client describing Jesus and his path towards completing his soul's mission upon the Earth.

C: I see four camels. I see Yeshua on one of them, and there's four of them leaving. Just like to spread the word to start the mission, or...the mission had already started but to really get it out there and spread the word, to start their journey. No fear. He actually...wow! What a...like his lack of fear of death, like it's exactly what I was talking about in this temple, and it's a really bright reflection on humanity and this timeline of forced medicalization and stuff like that. He's such a role model and it doesn't matter... He knew who he was. He knew he was going to be crucified; he knew he was going to be hated and he was just so solid in his truth and his commitment to the Light, and his commitment to God, and his commitment to truth, and his commitment to the truth of who he is. 'Cause it's really difficult to carry a truth that...yeah, it's nice and safe when your community hears you and believes in you, but to leave that security, to go out into the wolves and try, you know, to teach the wolves English is a very, very honorable...something I very much idolize in this very moment.

I see the heat. I see him sweating. I see him worn down. I see his hope. Like, it feels really hot on him, but I don't feel like it's...like the place he's at, I feel like it's symbolism.

M: Tell me more about that. So, he's worn down?

C: Yeah, like I said, there weren't very many beings of light like him, so the amount of hate versus the amount of love was just, you know...twenty to one. There just...

M: Sounds like it would have been really hard for him.

C: Yeah, and he was aware of this ending. He was aware of the odds. He was aware of all this. It's really interesting 'because I can feel his human aspect of it being really hard and him being tired, but I can feel his spirit, which was never tired, EVER! So, there's...I can see both aspects and very trusting, very willing to be a public symbol of...I'm going to say hate but being a public symbol of also not rolling over and being like "Okay, I'll stop being who I am. I'll stop trying to create peace in the world to save my human body." He was like not about that. The human body was just the experience in that NOW moment for his soul and he still connected to his soul that it never...that it didn't ever feel confusing to him.

Mary Magdalene

To know Yeshua and Mary Magdalene's true relationship, we can call into our awareness the path of Divine Partnership and Twin Flame souls. Yeshua and Mary met in their adolescent years. At the time, Mary was living in the chaos of the uninitiated world. Young Mary had a pure heart but was born into terrifying density. The collective consciousness at that time was negatively polarized and extremely low, steeped in fear and limitation. Society was patriarchal, and women were treated horribly. Tax collectors and religious dogma ruled the land, and the common consciousness was enslaved by fear and karma.

When Mary and Yeshua met, Yeshua was already very well into his studies and initiations. From the moment they met, he knew her as his Beloved, and her heart quickened in his presence. They spent sweet time in nature falling in love with one another as Yeshua shared the Mysteries with her. They practiced meditation and astral traveling together as he guided the Light of her True Nature out of the shadows of conditioned thinking and fear. Their innocent love illuminated both of them and propelled them on a rapid path of awakening and high alchemy.

Eventually, Yeshua and Mary made their way to Egypt, where Mary studied under the Holy Mother, Mother Mary, and learned the high priestess arts to become a priestess in the Ancient Egyptian Mystery Schools. Women gathered around Mother Mary to perform group rituals as they channeled divine cosmic energies into the ley lines of the Earth. They practiced moon rituals and womb magic and honored the esoteric power of their menstrual flow. Meanwhile, Yeshua and the other initiated men worked in the local communities to elevate the consciousness and protect the women while the women performed their sacred work.

Yeshua and Mary were Twin Flame partners united in marriage and in the light of their souls. One embodied the divine masculine, and the other embodied the divine feminine expression of perfected humanity. We cannot fully know one without knowing the other. We miss out on so much of the story without knowing the truth of Mary Magdalene and the Holy Mother. While Yeshua has received the global spotlight for his work on the Earth plane, it is Mary Magdalene who helped him fortify his determination and trust in his path and potential. When Jesus doubted his own abilities, it was Mary that comforted him back into his power.

Transcript: John the Beloved Comments on Mary and Jesus

John the Beloved, brother of Jesus and friend of Mary Magdalene shares his perspective of the dynamic relationship between Jesus and Mary.

C: *They were inseparable. They worked together all the time. When he laid a hand, she laid a hand. When he spoke, she curated the space, and when she spoke, he curated space. We followed her as much as we followed him. She also knew that she was reflecting an energy that was not quite time to be celebrated, but he celebrated her. We celebrated her through his example, but she also was celebrating him. They truly were one flesh. A mirror image. They would say that to us all the time; they both lived inside of everyone and that the masculine and feminine were not actually separate from one another. God is.*

Tantra: Sex Magic Alchemical Practices of Isis

When people describe Mary Magdalene in hypnosis sessions, they describe an exotic beauty with tanned olive skin, dark hair, and piercing eyes of love decorated with makeup in the style of Egyptian women. They comment on her captivating presence and her ability to fill a room with her powerful love vibration.

Mary Magdalene wore the serpent band of the priestesses of Isis around her arm as a mark of her path in the mystery school of the Temple of Isis. The Sex Magic practices of the Ancient Egyptian mystery schools and tantric traditions of India learned and practiced by Jesus and Mary were alchemical ascension practices done with a partner to clean the physical and subtle bodies so that one can access higher realms of consciousness existence. While making love, initiates could travel together in their light bodies and into Higher Realms of Light to study, heal, and expand in consciousness. The Egyptians saw these practices as divine technologies to access and embody the God/Goddess within.

Those who were not initiated into the sacred sexuality practices, regular people, would mistake this work as mere promiscuity and low morals because they see them through their cultural conditioning and limited understanding. Mary Magdalene was not an immoral whore but a powerful High Priestess of Alchemy and Magic. She was a master in her own right. Her wisdom and knowledge of high alchemy and tantric practices were instrumental in helping Yeshua develop the power of his Lightbody to hold the tremendous amount of Light needed to complete his public initiation on the cross.

Jesus and Mary were both practitioners of sacred sexuality and tantra. They used their sexual relationship to connect deeply with their Self, one another, and the Divine. This level of sacred sexual expression was not only shared between one another but shared with others to assist their awakening and ascension. I have had a client who described Mary and a group of women working together to cultivate erotic energy and sexual life force to heal from sexual trauma as well as a story of Jesus working with another man to help him move beyond his own sexual shadow and trauma. These two beings were masterfully empowered tantric practitioners who were completely liberated from religious and cultural conditionings. Many will read these words and reject them because of their own traumas and conditioning. Others will find these words comforting and liberating. We all carry sexual programming and wounding that limits our creative spirit and life force, and it is time for ascending humanity to peel away the layers of shame and condemnation and reclaim our soulful erotic innocence.

The Children of Jesus and Mary

I have not had a clear definitive answer to how many children Yeshua and Mary had together in my sessions. It ranges from one to four biological children that shared DNA from Yeshua and Mary. Jesus and Mary loved children, and many children would gather around them as they traveled and taught. At times, they would adopt children to take care of for some time.

When I asked about why there were discrepancies in the story regarding the number of children, I was told that the life of Jesus is presented differently depending on which timeline one is experiencing him through and there are infinite presentations of the life of Jesus and infinite ways the story played out and that we would benefit from expanding our understanding of holographic reality to understand the multidimensional presentation of his life.

The child most talked about was a girl named Sara. When four children are spoken of, clients describe two boys, one girl, and a perfectly balanced androgynous soul in a body with both sets of reproductive organs (an intersex, hermaphroditic human). This being was a prototype for future human generations. This was a genetic test to see if the new biology could handle such a highly evolved soul that embodied both masculine and feminine energies perfectly.

Sara is said to have been conceived through Light Conception by Mary just like Mother Mary did with Yeshua. The DNA from the offspring of Yeshua brought in an upgraded DNA signature. This DNA gave the body the ability to hold a higher light quotient than the other DNA signatures on the planet. People from this genetic lineage awaken easier and will develop psychic abilities faster than others. The offspring of Mary and Yeshua were protected by initiates. The new DNA signature was implanted into the collective gene pool through the following generations with the mixing of bloodlines across the planet.

Transcript: Rh-Negative Bloodlines

One somnambulistic client described the origins of Rh-negative blood types with this bloodline.

M: I'm wondering about this lineage of Jesus. What was the purpose of establishing a lineage?

C: Let me see... That lineage is one of the lineages, it could be the only one, but I think it could be one of the few people for whom the advanced skills are more acceptable. It's showing me copper blood, Rh-negative blood.

It carries light easier. Oh! Krissa has A negative. People can feed off light like a plant doing photosynthesis easier with Rh-negative. It's less dense; it's less earth-bound, crystalline. These people are heralds or will be evolving faster into what eventually the whole of humanity can be. So, these people can show the way and also help calm the fear because people get so fearful when things are changing. These people can show, "Hey, what we're going through isn't so bad."

And there are some individuals on the planet now who can subsist almost solely on breath, light, and maybe some juice. That's actually the evolving direction. Jesus's lineage seeded some humans on this planet with not only Rh-negative, but that's one of the strongest manifestations; it's just a less dense, less earth-bound blood type. It's a lineage of people holding the higher Light frequency.

Traveling and Spreading Knowledge

Yeshua and Mary traveled together to many distant places to share and trade knowledge. Yeshua's uncle, Joseph of Arimathea, also an Essene high initiate, was an extremely wealthy tin tradesman. He would purchase tin ore from his brethren, the Druids, in the UK and sell it to harbors in the Mediterranean and distant waters.

His wealth, seafaring ships, and connections along the various trade routes across the Middle East, Asia, and Europe gave the Essene community the ability to travel great distances. Yeshua traveled to Avalon (Glastonbury and Wales) to study with the Druids, India to study with the yoga masters, Tibet to study with Buddhist monastics, the Far East to study with the Chinese masters, and likely other areas. Often Mary was by his side. These two traveled to more places than we can imagine, all the while knowing that time was limited and there was much to do and share.

Large groups of people followed them wherever they went to hear the wisdom and knowledge they shared. They barely had time alone. While they were a healing presence, they also shook things up with their advanced ideas of a liberated consciousness. Often, they were weary and tired because they would flee from one town to the next under cover of nightfall because authorities were looking for them. This even included being arrested or detained because they were seen as radical and dangerous by power authorities.

Too often, I hear people using the life of Jesus as a whipping tool. One of the major issues that I hear people talk about is that Jesus did not charge for his healing. He gave it away, and so, as healers, we should not charge for healing services since it is not "Christlike." Jesus's ministry was funded and supported by his uncle. Yeshua, Mary Magdalene, and other disciples would ride on the various seafaring ships owned by Joseph to distant ports in Greece, Turkey, India, Britain, the Far East, and likely other distant lands to not only trade goods but to trade knowledge with other wise people. Jesus did not need to "charge" for services because he had a patron and many galactic and higher dimensional allies directly (and financially) supporting his path.

The Ministry: Spreading the Word

The disciples of Jesus extended beyond the core twelve. They were made of men and women from the Essene community and other followers who believed in the teachings of Jesus. Jesus and his disciples traveled together for a few years to teach Oneness and heart-based devotional living. They taught of the Light within and how to become a sovereign soul, free from the slavery of a conditioned mind and the Truth of Eternal Living. Even after his crucifixion and resurrection, many disciples paid the price with their lives as they continued to spread "the good news" of Ascension and God's promise of a New Earth.

Miraculous Healing

Essene community members were taught methods of natural healing and advanced energy healing practices. Jesus and the disciples traveled together, spreading The Word (Truth from the Higher Realms) and performing many healings across the land. These highly advanced spiritual humans could "read the soul" of the person to see the root cause of the illness. If it aligned with the individual's soul pathway and did not interfere with the free will of that soul's choice to learn through suffering, rapid multidimensional healing would be performed through psychic transmission, laying of hands, and other healing practices. When complete healing could not be done, natural herbal remedies were used to support the healing process and relieve suffering. This included frankincense, myrrh, and eucalyptus, commonly used and readily available in the Middle East.

One of the higher mystery teachings involved resurrecting the dead. I have had two different clients describe a scene in a temple where Jesus, Mary, and a few other initiates were present. They stood around a fire made of blue flames and began calling on the presence of God to reanimate a dead calf that lay on the floor. They describe a Light power descending into the calf, bringing it back to life. You can imagine what it was like to hear this story once. It was extra wild to hear the same scene described by another person a year later. These transcriptions are presented later in this manuscript.

Another client went to the lifetime of John the Beloved, brother of Yeshua. When John was just a young boy, he became sick with an illness that drained him of life force energy until he died. As he transitioned into the Light, he was united with his spiritual family and higher consciousness. He heard the voice of his brother Yeshua calling out his name, and the next thing he knew, he was back in his body in the tomb with Yeshua by his side shining a brilliant grin. Like many people with Near Death Experiences (NDEs), John returned with expanded consciousness and was invited to join his brother on his travels to be his scribe. John the Beloved eventually writes the original scriptures that would become the Book of Revelations.

I had a hypnosis session where a client described Yeshua kneeling over the body of a woman who had just passed. Yeshua connected with the soul's higher consciousness and coordinated an exchange with the body, a walk-in. As the tired soul of the body left the Earth plane, another fresh portion of the oversoul was invited back into the body to reanimate it. The body was resurrected with a new consciousness with a higher frequency to continue in service to awakening with the new vibration. Walk-ins are a common way for members of the Hierarchy of Light to embody for a short time to accomplish their work to support the Higher Evolutionary Design and Trajectory.

Judas: Devout Disciple of Yeshua

Those closest to Yeshua knew that at some point he would have to leave the Earth plane. Not everyone knew all the details, but they were told many times that those days would come. When asked who was most faithful, most rooted in nondual awareness, to do what was necessary to lead the authorities to Jesus, Judas volunteered. Yeshua and Judas both knew what needed to happen. Even though Judas struggled with his role after volunteering, his role was incredibly essential and blessed by the Divine.

In these modern times, we have many Judas characters in our human collective who, on the soul level, agreed to come into the Earth to play the role of the villain and move us into our own resurrection timeline. These souls will play out terrible actions that will assist the human collective in shifting out of their slave mind and into the power of the heart by creating conditions that inherently invite us to reach for higher wisdom and higher love.

Rites of the Sepulcher: Initiation on the Cross

The Rites of the Sepulcher performed by Jesus have roots in Ancient Egypt and Ancient Tibet. High-level initiates in these orders would use these practices to reverse the aging process of the body and access higher realms of Light and Wisdom.

During this process, the body would go into a state of dormancy and appear dead. Often these bodies would be stored in tombs or hidden caves for safety. In this meditative state, the soul traveled to higher realms while remaining tethered to the body through a chord of Light. Once the soul was ready to reenter the body, the tending priest or priestess would be notified psychically and begin working with the soul and body to help the soul integrate and reanimate the body. The soul would reenter the body with a tremendous amount of Light and higher coding that would regenerate the body's cells so that the body would reverse its aging process. Initiates could do this process repeatedly, extending their life by hundreds of years. Once the initiate was finished with their Earthly experience, they would stop performing the rites and allow the body to die. Many ancient traditions speak of this rite, particularly in the Tibetan mystery schools where young Jesus studied.

While on the cross, Yeshua remained tethered to his body as his soul traveled to the higher realms back to Source. In my sessions, many speak of his Lightbody emerging from the cross and the coordinated efforts by Joseph of Arimathea and others to move him to a close tomb paid for by Joseph. While in the tomb, the completion of the Rite of the Sepulcher was performed. When Yeshua's soul returned to his body, he brought the keys to our Ascension given to him by Source. He broke through the density of the Earth realm's dark matrix created by fallen thoughtforms and the influence of negative polarity beings and paved the way for humanity to connect again and collaborate with the higher realms. His body was transformed into the Christ Light body, and he was no longer limited to the Earth plane. At will, he could take his body to the higher realms and travel to other star systems.

This is what humanity is transforming into. This is our destiny! As he said, "You will do these things and more!" We are also passing through our own initiations to purify our souls so that the Christ Consciousness Light can move through our bodies. When this "Event" happens, we will no longer be limited to the Earth plane. We will be co-creators with the Hierarchies of Light and our Star Nation brethren. We will travel throughout Creation, tend to the many Gardens, and teach The Way of Light and Love.

Post Resurrection

Quickly after the crucifixion, many of those who followed Jesus and the Ministry were in danger from the authorities. Mary and other family members and disciples fled Israel to escape punishment and death. They met up with other Essenes and initiates who guided them to safety. Some of the group split partway and made their way to Egypt/Africa, and Mary, John, Sara, and others made their way to Southern France to a community of allies. For more information on these fractals of the Ministry, check out the Coptic Gnostic Christian and Saint Thomas Christian history.

After the resurrection, Yeshua continued to teach the disciples before finally ascending to the Heavens. For an account of his teachings, I highly suggest the *Pistis Sophia* translated by Dr. J.J. Hurtak.

Jesus was a human, just like you and me. Through yogic and alchemical practices, he realized his Divine Nature. His life is something to aspire to but not something that we should use to punish ourselves or perpetuate self-loathing or reinforce our slave mentality. His life is a perfect example of what human potential is. If you want to know the hidden mysteries, invite Jesus into your heart. Invite Mary into your heart. Invite the Holy Family into your heart. Ask them to show you the Christ That Lives Within You. Let them help you open your heart and teach you The Way of Love and Light.

Religions

The Word, the original religion of the Multiverse, is the pure Light, Love, and Unity coding of Creation. It lives within your very heart and has the power to illuminate and transform every atom of your being. In the ancient times of the high consciousness civilization of Lemuria, The Word was what we radiated into the environment of Gaia from our beingness. When the negative polarity was permitted by Source to enter the Earth realm, Truth, Light, and Love began to become distorted. In doing so, humanity's commitment to living a noble and righteous life has been tested for countless generations.

While there are certainly positively polarized religious leaders throughout time, religions, for the most part, have been used by the colonizing shadow forces, those in service-to-self consciousness, to distort spiritual teachings as an attempt to control human consciousness. This experiment in consciousness is ending as we reach the graduation point and the culmination of this Grand Redemption Plan, and all that is hidden will be brought into the Light.

Yeshua ben Joseph and the disciples of the ministry dedicated their teaching and their lives to uplift and empower people in their Divine Creatorship. They taught people that they held the keys to the Kingdom of Heaven. They taught Love, union with the Divine, and heart-centered living. Jesus did not want to be the center of religion but wanted us to find the Living Power of the Divine within us and all of Life.

Religion is something outside of the body and is part of the *maya*, or illusion, of Creation. It is temporary. It will decay and wither away. Some components of the *maya* of religion trap people in cycles of suffering such as messages of fear and damnation, while some of the *maya* of religions assist in the liberation of consciousness such as messages of higher love and images of divine beings that remind people of the presence of God.

From a reincarnation perspective, religious institutions are schools of evolution for a soul to experience itself through the lens of that religion's beliefs. There are many paths, and all paths are valid and lead to Source-realization eventually. Every drop of water eventually makes its way to the ocean. The illuminated Truth of the Love and Light of Source is found in all the world's wisdom traditions and religions. No one religion owns the way to Source.

Much of what modern Institutional Christianity teaches are teachings that have been distorted or fabricated to program and control people using fear, judgment, and punishment. The Spanish Inquisition and witch trials aimed to eliminate the mystery teachings, magical traditions, and mystical peoples of the world and convert people to their twisted version of Christ's teachings. This all served a higher purpose to catalyze collective humanity out of slave mentality. When we are finished with enslaving our consciousness, we will no longer need tyrannical external authority figures and institutions. All of the suffering has been an invitation to uncover the tyranny of the mind and open to the limitlessness of our being and Source.

The choice has always been left to the individual and to the collective of humanity to follow the truth within our hearts or follow a concept of God given to us by someone else. The externalized religions of the world reflect our collective denial of our divinity and power. Many Christians worldwide are leaving organized religion to cultivate a living relationship with the love of Christ that is free from dogma, shame, and fear. Simultaneously, people who have never involved themselves with a religion of any kind are using the teachings of Christ to improve the quality of their own life.

Jesus and the teachings of the Ascended Masters show us the way of Love and Unity. Jesus is quoted in the Bible as saying, "I am the resurrection and the life. The one who believes in me will live, even though they die." Jesus was speaking of the path of ascension. He was speaking about awakening to our divinity and the truth that we never truly die. He offered an invitation for the human collective to release the fears and slave mentality of lower consciousness and expand into new horizons of consciousness and unity. To "believe in Him" is to believe in the truth of ascension and the promise of God to grant ascension to our generation.

Feel into the essence of Jesus's teachings and feel the vibration of unconditional love that illuminates his words and speaks to your heart. Let this Light permeate every cell of your being and awaken the Divinity that YOU ARE. Drop the dogma and align with the great power and potential he embodied.

He asked his followers to follow in his footsteps and share the "good news" of everlasting life and this new age's dawning. We each have been given an invitation to awaken and serve humanity as ambassadors of Light and Unity.

The Threefold Flame of the Heart

The Threefold Flame of the Heart is the divine spark located within the central chamber of the heart's altar, the inner sanctum. The three flames represent three sublime virtues of a Christ-conscious being: Wisdom, Power, and Love. Wisdom is the application of the mind to Higher Wisdom and Divine Truth and the illumination that comes from the right use of spiritual knowledge. Power is seen as the right use of our willpower to be in service to healing and awakening others to the Christ that dwells within. Through our allowing, Universal Love works through us so that we can be instruments of selfless service for the Greater Good for All.

To be born again is to be resurrected from spiritual death by pursuing spiritual growth and the absorption of spiritual wisdom into your being. Through spiritual practices, we evolve beyond our animalistic, carnal nature into a spiritual human being of Divine Light, a divine-human synthesis. The path of embodying our Holy Christ Self involves loving ourselves completely, and in doing so, we emanate love to all we meet. As we dissolve the conditioning of our mind and surrender to the inner voice of love, we reveal our own Christhood.

It is up to each of us to cultivate a deeply personal relationship with the Unconditional Love and Grace of Source. The potential for attaining the Christ-Self, the Buddha-Self, or the Krishna-Self is available for ALL who wish to grow in Truth and Love. Bless us all!

TWO

Protector of Jesus

This client came into the first scene of a vast golden desert with structures, temples, and pyramids. The client saw herself as a male human in his twenties wearing a white, shin-length robe with gold trim and a draping over his head. He was walking through a corridor with pillars and arrived at a feast with other people. Everyone's attention was on a "loud and boisterous" woman who was feeding everyone who he called Maria. Not much information was coming from this scene, so I moved the client forward to the next important scene.

NEXT SCENE: IN A TOMB

C: *I'm in a tomb, a pyramid, or temple...but it's deep, enclosed. There's writing on the walls, and there's something protected in the center. It feels like a pyramid. I'm scribing. I'm reading something off the walls. The history of this place...there's something that I'm trying to find out there, something coded there that I'm in search of. There are other people here, but I'm walking around, keeping to myself, and scribing the symbols that I'm seeing.*

M: **Why are you looking for this code?**

C: *It's connected to what I'm learning. It's something I'm being guided to learn. I'm leaving there, and I'm walking out into the bright sun. It's very bright outside. I'm going to some water, a river, and I'm releasing something down the river. They're like tubes of gold filled with paper. I'm letting them go and sending them somewhere. Something about a child. Whatever I'm sending down the river is related to a child, and I expect that someone will receive them.*

M: **What's important about this child that you are sending information down the stream?**

C: *This child is special. This child is a teacher, very wise, and there's something that I've scribed to be kept for that child. He's come to teach and to help us in this place understand what I was writing, what wisdom and information I was collecting. I've known he was coming.*

M: **How did you know he was coming?**

C: I have a teacher that told me what to do and told me about the child. I am a student of this teacher and doing my part.

NEXT SCENE: SEEING THE CHILD

C: I see the child now. He's young, maybe seven or eight. I'm there with his mother, and he's just playing. He's very quiet. His mother is watching our interaction. I've come to share what I know about him with her. She knows he's special, and she's grateful, listening, and observing him as am I. I share that he is going to play a really important role in the freeing of people and ending corruption where we live. He can see a lot more than most people can see. He can foresee things. He has the power to predict what is going to happen. He plays a very important role in the turning of the times. I tell her to not be afraid. He will have to leave, and he will be on his own path. I tell her to encourage him to be brave as well. The boy seems to know everything already that I'm sharing with his mother. He seems to understand.

NEXT SCENE: TURMOIL AND CHAOS

C: There's busyness and turmoil. A lot of chaos in the streets of this place. There are horses and chariots, a lot of shouting and commotion. It feels like a sort of political unrest; the people are upset about something — their leaders or hierarchical beings that have upset people. There's revolt. I'm observing the scene, and it's like I'm always collecting data wherever I am. Just being there, observing whatever is happening, but I feel calm. They're bringing up that boy. He's more grown now. I think they're trying to arrest him. They bring him out; there's a crowd of people. He's still quiet, and I don't know why they're arresting him. I think his power has been found out. I see some people in the crowd that I recognize that are also peaceful, and we meet eyes. There are also others like me that are peaceful and observing. It feels like we are anchoring Light there. And I observe the boy, he's now grown, he's more of a man. I don't fear because I know that he's always okay.

The people are watching the man get arrested, but he's up above them on a platform so they can see. He's thin. Healthy but thin. He has dark hair, long hair, and he's peaceful. He's not fighting back or speaking. There's a lot of people watching and shouting. It's like a very public display of arrest for some reason.

M: What color is his skin?

C: It's dark, but not black. Tan, olive-like skin. I feel this might be Jesus. It might be where they're choosing what to do with him. They've arrested him, and they're asking people what to do with him. People are shouting and this man, let's call him Jesus, they're accusing him because of his power, his clairvoyance. They ask the crowd and decide to crucify him. This is the scene. It's very loud, and there are many people. They're all turning against him. He's a healer and sees through the distorted powers that are in charge, and he speaks of that, and they don't like it.

They're taking him away. They're pulling him; his hands are tied. They're taking him away to have him murdered. He's been sentenced. There are some people that are really sad; they're crying and know it's not right. There are many others that are very angry, very aggressive people; most of them are following, it's like it's a spectacle of some kind. It's disturbing. People are very unkind. I stay behind and continue to follow and observe what's happening. I keep noticing the beings in the crowd that are aware of me, and I'm aware of them. We are there, but again, it's almost like we're invisible. We're quiet.

M: How do you know these people?

C: We all feel like we're not from Earth. We feel like angels, and we've come knowing our role here now. We are anchoring Light and observing and recording even just by our observing of what's happening.

NEXT SCENE: THE CRUCIFIXION

C: (Begins to cry) I'm there now where they've crucified him. It's a very sad day. It feels very sad...the land, the people, everything is sad. I see his mother and two other women; they're crying, and they don't want to leave. Many people have already left. They're there with him and don't want to leave. It's raining a little now; it's stormy. Very surreal. The energy is very surreal. I'm approaching his mother again. We don't speak words; we just communicate with our eyes. There are no words. She's very sad, but she's also very strong. I feel a sensation of really warm, tingling sensations in my shoulders and in my back. I'm there to help these three women come down the mountain, come down the hill, and care for them. It feels like the energy is very potent, and it's uncertain what will happen, and I want to make sure they're safe.

M: What can you tell me about these women and your connection to them?

C: I have a strong connection to his mother. I'm a protector of her. The other two women she's very close with; they're very special, and they were special to him. He asked me to protect them. They're all Mary. They have to move now. They're being guided to move...they may not be safe. The people in power, they want to control and know everything, and now that he's gone, they may want to control his family, people that knew him and knew who he was, who he is. So, they have to move away. There are many of us that are helping them move away. Take them to a safe place, for now; they've sort of been hiding. But we're not far from where his body will be because they want to stay close with him.

M: What is everyone talking about as you go into hiding?

C: There are not many words. There's a lot of communicating without words. As we move, we want to be very quiet, not because we don't want to be heard, there are many people out and about, but words feel limiting to what's happening, truly. I have been reassuring them that they're safe. A lot of people have left the mountain, and a lot of sorrow then comes. The commotion has gone, and it's like the family is left with the weight, and his body is put into the tomb, and no one seems to care anymore. The family is very sad. There are others that are close to him that come, gather together, and stay close. There were men that prepared the body. We didn't stay to watch. And they put the body in a tomb, but Mary wants to see the tomb, see the body. So, I'm agreeing to take them there. Yeah, this is when...

NEXT SCENE: GOING TO THE TOMB

M: What do you see?

C: We can't go there yet. We can't go there now, but I agreed to take them when it's right. The sun is out now; the weather has changed. It's hot. It's feeling very important that we stay hidden now. We walk to the tomb. For days we walk there. This is when we find the tomb empty. It's empty. There's the cloth there that he was wrapped in. The tomb is empty, and there is some panic. There's some fear and panic. This is when Mary wanders off, and she sees him. She's the first to see him. She sees his Lightbody. He has risen. She sees him, and she cries and screams. We find her, and she tells us she has seen him. She knew she would see him. She knew what would happen.

M: Which Mary is this that sees him?

C: This is Mary...not his mother, this is Mary Magdalene. His beloved. One of the Mary Magdalenes. It's very prayerful now. There's relief, and we are listening to Mary, what she saw. What she understands is to not fear that he is here, and they must move, and he is with them.

M: Are you all aware of how he was able to change into this Lightbody?

C: He prepared a long time for this. This is what the initiates were preparing for and Mary specifically with Jesus — preparing for the Lightbody resurrection.

M: What happens next? What do you learn?

C: We learn that there are many things set in place for the family to move. To be safe, they will travel across the sea. They've prepared to go on a voyage now. To be safe, I will stay. I am staying. There are men in their family that take them to safety into a boat, and they go where they know they'll be safe. I don't know where they're going...they're going across the sea. I stay. I feel that my role has been fulfilled to let them go, and there is still a lot happening here that I have to stay here.

M: What do you do next?

C: I go back. I go back to the city where things are more quiet now, but there's a lot of...the energy is very unsettled here. That's part of my work here, to balance the energy. People are scattering away; people are going home, back to where they live. It just feels very unsettled in this place, so people are leaving.

NEXT SCENE: WRITING THE KNOWLEDGE

C: I am old now. I am old, and I am writing down many things — books, and books. Writing...I feel near the end of my time on Earth, and I am writing what I've experienced and what I know. My wisdom.

M: Tell me about it. What are you writing?

C: It's related to the wisdom and knowledge I was gathering in my younger years, and there are also predictions of what will come. I'm writing to help people understand what has happened in this time, around my family and my teacher and this boy and the life of Jesus and his mother. It feels important that I write everything down because I may not be living here much longer.

M: I would like to know more about the history of your relationship with Mother Mary. Let's go back to the first time you met her.

NEXT SCENE: MEETING MOTHER MARY

C: The first time I saw her was before she knew she would be a mother. I knew who she was. She was gathering water. I just observed her. I didn't speak with her this time; it wasn't time. I was even protecting her then, making sure she was safe and well. She was...she was happy and safe and very gentle. Very present.

M: Let's move forward to the next time you saw Mary.

C: Now I'm with her when she knows she's pregnant. She's scared; she's crying. Again, she's crying, but she's strong.

M: What does she know about this pregnancy?

C: He was Light conceived by her. She was an initiate. A very pure being, very strong and devoted in her life, in her practice, and she was told she would carry a son into the world. She's scared because she doesn't feel ready. She doesn't know she's ready. There's a part of her that knows she's ready...she's human now, and she's scared. She doesn't know all of who he is yet. She knows he's special and important.

M: Can you share with me about Light conception and what you know about this process?

C: Yes. Light conception is very possible with devoted practice. Humans have forgotten. It's not possible with all, but with some. It is to be conceived by the energy of Light. This is why they called her a Virgin. It's that purity of Light to be able to conceive and that energy to be able to bring a physical being into form through the Light.

NEXT SCENE: THE BIRTH OF JESUS

C: I was there when he was born. It was so beautiful. The scene was so peaceful. There are a few people, many animals there, beings that could hold the frequency of him coming into form. There was a lot of Light there. Very peaceful. It was also somewhat hidden away, somewhat secretive. Not secret but protected. And there were many celestial beings present as well. So many celestial beings came for the birth. There were many starlight beings in the sky. It was a very bright night. The energy was very angelic, very light, as it had to be for him to come. Even now, I feel a spinning sensation; I feel a swirling of energy of Light. I feel the power of the energy that night. It was an energy that the Earth had not felt in a very long time. Mary is very happy, very at peace, very supported, which makes me happy.

M: Let's learn a little bit more. Can you tell me about this star in the sky?

C: The star of Bethlehem is his home. A ship. It did guide beings to this place; it was not just a star. It is a ship where Jesus and Mary came from, and it is present along with others and legions of angels and star beings. It was quite an event in the heavens.

M: Can you tell me more about how Jesus and Mary came from the ship? What do you know about it?

C: The ship...there are Pleiadian ties, but it is not just a Pleiadian ship. It is from beyond there, but it did travel through the Pleiades to come there as well.

M: How were Mary and Jesus able to get from that ship and into these bodies?

C: That is the Light conception. Yes, it's possible with the help of the energies and technologies of these ships, and from this ship, in particular. And with communication and connection with beings on the Earth, it is possible.

NEXT SCENE: YOUNG JESUS

C: I'm back to the time when he was seven or eight years old. I spent time with him then to make sure that Jesus was in a safe place and protected, but also that they were happy and well. It's important that they felt that at this time. Mary was well taken care of; they had a good community, and Jesus was very, very wise, very bright — learning a lot and teaching. He was very interested in what was happening in the temples, what was being taught to the people. He had innate wisdom about spirituality and what he was learning was the human way of things, what was happening here, and why and who was controlling and teaching. He did not fear. He was not capable of certain emotions, so he was very bold in his learning and his speech when he chose to speak. Often, he was quiet. Very sweet boy.

NEXT SCENE: JESUS AND MARY MAGDALENE

C: Now, Jesus is grown, and he has many people around him almost all the time, still teaching and healing. He's learning still...he's learning with Mary Magdalene. They see their role in each other's lives, and they're very devoted. They travel energetically together; they strengthen their energies together, and they teach this among a small group of them, family, what we call disciples. And he's healing many people. His presence is healing; he doesn't need to do much. His presence, everywhere he goes, is healing. He knows this, and he travels. He teaches as he travels.

M: How do they travel together energetically and strengthen their energies?

C: They practice mastering their physical body with the breath. Moving their energy together strengthens the Ka body, the energetic body. They learn from a long line of initiates, and Jesus learns much of this from Mary, Mary Magdalene. All three Marys and many others who are all family, they learn these practices, and it's just breath. It is physical with their bodies as well as with their minds; they go into their bodies; they breathe. They build the energy; they move the energy; and the more they do this, the more they do it easily and quickly. This strengthens Jesus for his path.

NEXT SCENE: THE CHRIST BLOODLINE

C: Children. There's a lot of children with him. There's a lot of children born at this time. Many people in their lineage, bloodline, in their family. He's teaching many children. There's much to be carried on. He knows these children will understand and carry. It's important that they carry codes and wisdom. Children come to him. Those that are meant to carry the codes know to come to him. Their parents bring them from all over.

M: Share with me about the bloodline and family.

C: This bloodline, they're all connected from the stars, from beyond here on Earth. They know each other from far back, from beyond, and incarnate many times to carry this wisdom and these codes. Oftentimes secretly, quietly to maintain the presence of this Light on Earth. There is a lot of corruption. There is a lot of hiding the truth, what we know now as religions, and it's important that this bloodline be carried, mostly quietly, and so it's time.

M: Who works with these children? How does he share this information with the children?

C: There is activation happening. He doesn't need to say very much. Spending time with these children is activating them, and they remember. Mostly it just looks like loving play, being in nature, and laughing and eating food together. Mostly he uses energy, not words.

NEXT SCENE: JESUS STRUGGLES

C: Jesus is struggling. He's not sick, but he's tired. Doubt, he's feeling his humanness; he's feeling tired and somewhat confused. These are the times that Mary strengthens him and reminds him. He has a deep respect for her and her wisdom.

She strengthens him, his body, and his spirit. There weren't many times that he fell to this lower vibration, but when he did, it was very important that she was there to strengthen him, and she was.

NEXT SCENE: RESURRECTED JESUS

C: *This is where Jesus is resurrected. He has risen into his Lightbody. He's coming in and out now, space and time at will, and he comes in and out to assist. To visit. To visit his family, to visit only where it is truly important for him to be visible and present. To fulfill his path on Earth.*

M: Tell me what's happening. What is he doing?

C: *He mostly appears to his mother and Mary Magdalene and other Essenes. He continues to teach them to guide their path. He brings peace and continues to anchor peace. He's teaching them how to do it. It's done. He's teaching them his full experience now that he has resurrected, so they can know how to do this.*

M: What does he teach them? How does he do it?

C: *They have very strict, devoted nutritional practices. Water. Water is very important — healthy water. And using the breath and body as a tool for ascension. Knowing the body, knowing the technology of the body, which takes just practice. We know...his teaching is that we have the wisdom within us. It's just devotion and practice. Being healthy, healthy in our bodies.*

M: What does he share about being the Way and the Light?

C: *There's love. The way is love; it is. It is who we are, we know. It sounds so simple, but it is so simple. He shows that there is nothing that can hurt us or what he is saying...there is only love. There truly is only love, and when we are in our bodies, we experience this love, this ecstasy, this blissful feeling that is love. And the more we are in that place, the less allowed all other feelings are in our bodies.*

We just need to practice being in love. It takes practice. It's not easy. Sometimes it's compassion, for ourselves too, for ourselves. He also teaches that the Way is living. Living in love, living as an example, living without separation, we have less separation as human beings. We are all connected; we are all one. He teaches to remember that. So much pain is caused by separation, by polarity, that's so created by man.

And greed, he teaches to give. Forgive. He teaches forgiveness, it all comes back to giving. Giving our love in all forms, in all that we have. The more we give, we receive.

THREE

John the Beloved

I first had the opportunity to work with Erik when I began learning quantum healing hypnosis. This is another one of those sessions where I felt like I was riding a bucking bronco of energy! It may have been the first session where a client experienced a lifetime in Atlantis, and it was the first time Jesus made a guest appearance!

As I moved Erik to the next scene, he began sobbing uncontrollably. The room began to rise in frequency, and I began to sweat. Something different was happening. As he began to talk, I had to consciously deepen my breath to stay focused. A lot of energy was moving.

C: *I am seeing something that looks like walking on sandy earth before the cross. My teacher is being hanged.*

M: Who was your teacher?

C: *Yeshua ben Joseph (begins to sob). Yeshua ben Joseph. Yeshua ben Joseph...*

M: How does it feel to be with your teacher as he dies there?

C: *Devastating (crying).*

M: I want you to scan around and see if there is anybody who has more information for you there. Tell me what you're experiencing.

C: *Angry.*

M: What are you angry about?

C: *That no one can see this beauty, that they are so afraid of their own truth that they had to destroy.*

M: To destroy what? Tell me what you are hearing.

C: *His Lightbody has emerged from the cross, and he is standing before me. My heart. His eyes. See the way I do see. Nothing is lost or destroyed; the flesh is but a temporary experience, and all experience is joyful to the consciousness that brings life into it. He says when you learn to stop looking for me, for the teacher or the love to save you, then you shall see what I see when I look upon you.*

M: And what do you see when you look upon us?

C: *Children learning to walk. Delightful in their stumble. Sweet in their ignorance, their curiosity. Innocent.*

M: It sounds like you have a deep love for us.

C: (Deep crying).

M: Yeshua, I would like you to help our dear friend here, and as you're visiting with us, today offer him some healing.

Yeshua: Feed my sheep. Tend to my flock. Walk in the glory of my name.

M: There is a lot of conflict in our modern world about who you were and the messages you brought, and what we should do to really be like Christ. Can you tell us what that is? What it's really like to be Christlike?

Yeshua: It is like the most simple way to be. Everything complicated, and the perception of complication is no longer interesting. When it is accepted, it is a beautiful game, as an intellectual stimulus perhaps, to explore complications, but as we come to be addicted to the sense of value and worth that we believe comes from the complication of creating difficult and complex problems that require complex solutions and that garners the value and worth that allows us to seemingly assimilate a deserving, what we're begging for. When this interest, preoccupation, that the idea of value and worth through complication ceases, and the simplicity of the moment is unopposed in its majesty… That is what it's like to be Christ. A child of God that is the fullness of God that has been liberated from the connection and idea of pain.

That [Christ, a child of God] looks upon the Kingdom of Heaven on Earth with a single eye [nondual consciousness] and notices that even as the resistance believes that it is falling from heaven, that it is fighting against, rejecting its very nature, it is still hurtling its way home. When you learn to hear that one message, no matter what is spoken, that is when you find Christ.

I wanted to learn more about the story. Several months later, Erik and I worked together again to focus on the lifetime of John the Beloved. Here is what we discovered!

C: We're walking along a river in the desert. Actually, I am seeing myself as a young boy. There's a caravan. It feels the whole family, like a lot of families, are filing into another city for the census. We're being counted. We're also going to be visiting another family.

M: Look down at the ground and tell me what you're wearing as you scan up the body. Tell me what you notice about the body you're in.

C: It's small. Small and maybe ten or eleven, and I'm wearing ankle links and a vest-like robe and an undergarment with sandals.

M: How do your emotions feel?

C: Excited.

M: What are you excited about?

C: Getting to see my older brother. Yeah, he's going to meet up with us in Jerusalem. We're in the home of my father's brother, my uncle. There's a large wooden table with lots of people talking and waiting for my brother to come. He's been away in India and Egypt and other places studying. My uncle, my dad, and my uncle, but mostly my uncle, paid for him to go. So, we're just here to honor my uncle and to welcome my brother back and hear about his experiences. I love him so much. I've missed him, and he's been gone for a couple of years or so. I am anxious to see him.

M: You said that your mom and your dad and your uncle are there. Who else is there?

C: My uncle's wife and their children and my mother's father and her sisters and my one other brother and two sisters and some servant people.

M: Tell me what happens next.

C: He arrives.

M: How does it feel? What's it like?

C: His hair is longer, and he's smiling and hugging my father. They embrace for a long time, and then my mother. Then my brothers and sisters. We're just sitting on the floor all eating, and there's singing now. We're singing a very old Jewish song of homecoming, celebration, and the feast. He comes over to me and asks where I am, and I say, "Here I am." He picks me up. His hands are warm, and it feels like tingling throughout my whole body. He asks if I can feel it, and I nod my head. I don't know why exactly I have tears in my eyes (emotional).

M: Feel into it. What are those tears about?

C: I don't know. He says there's much for me to learn and that one day I will travel with him, and I will get to go on the journey too. He hugs me and kisses my mouth and says, "Let's enjoy the feast." and puts me down.

M: Does he share anything about his time from his travels?

C: The family is eager to hear about the exotic lands we had only heard about. He is really reluctant to share. He says that he found ancient civilizations and the ability to travel through time and that he can feel his teachers with him always. It sounds fantastical. Some of the women ask about not having to go to the temple in order to meet teachers. He is saying the teachers are within his consciousness. Then he is talking about food and the True Nourishment, that which is nourishing. Some of the people are laughing now, in a fantastical way. My mother and father are sitting on either side of him, and they feel proud, and they know. They are assured something is profoundly meant for him to be.

NEXT SCENE: JOHN BECOMES ILL

C: I'm sick. It's about five years later. I'm becoming a man. I've become ill, and they do not know what is causing the illness. I am sweating and trembling and vomiting. My body goes into seizures, and then I seem to go unconscious.

M: What is your experience during this?

C: Fear. Immense fear and anger. Mainly that I haven't seen my brother again in quite a long time and I've been waiting to get older for him to come for a visit again and to say it's time for me to go with him, and it hasn't happened yet. I am angry that I may be dying here, and I'm not going to be able to see him again.

M: I see why that would be upsetting.

C: My mother is with me. She is rubbing my cheek and my hand. She is very calm, with gentle tears. She's telling me to rest and be at peace. Be at peace. I don't want to; I want to fight. I want to stay. I want to see him again, but it's no use. Everything goes dark and black. I feel my body tightening, going hard.

M: What happens now?

C: I'm in the spirit plane with angels all around...watercolors, vibrant. I hear trumpets and horns and string instruments and singing. I feel large. There is intimate golden light as myself, in myself. This fabric that everything is, that the angels are a part of, and I feel I remember that the largest part of my soul essence had not yet entered John's young body and that it will soon re-enter. I can now see the tomb and see his body wrapped and laid in there. Such beautiful music and beautiful light. I watch the tomb open, and my brother enters. He's dressed all in white, and he lays his hands upon the body, and I am rejoicing. Praise. The very sound of the trumpets, I am the Light that precedes the angels' presence, and he commands my reentry in the body, reanimation, and I am aware and profoundly devoted. I, as the Breath of Life, reenter, merge, activate. "John!" He's commanding me to rise up to open my eyes. To stand. To walk. To speak. To praise. He leads me out of the tomb into the light. My sister, aunt, and mother are there, and they weep and gasp and shout. My brother calms them, then they rush over to me and are hugging me and splashing me with water.

My brother smiles and says it's time. He announces to them that I am to be by his side from now on.

M: Is anything different now that you are back in your body?

C: Everything is different. Now I know the truth of death and life. Now I know that everything is true and that there's no more waiting. No more confusion. No more anger, at least not in the way I felt it before. Now I feel ordained and devoted, curious, but also immensely powerful. Part of it is feeling chosen by or protected by or in the wake of his energy, and some part of me knows there's much left to be done, to experience, to unravel, to integrate in my own consciousness. In these moments after reawakening, I am very close in his energy, like an extension of his energy field. I am getting a glimpse of the authority and the majesty and the grace that he is, that I am, but that's been still perceived as bestowed upon me, not that which I am, like is in his energy. So simultaneous awareness of the truth of being and also the great leap of consciousness that very quickly was accelerated through the seeming death and resurrection of the body to the greater shift in consciousness beyond the body that simply symbolized how much, how many more rooms of this great palace (the multiverse) have yet to be explored or touched by my own personal vantage point. How glorious the journey is to become, to be. Yes.

M: Beautiful.

C: I go with him. We leave almost immediately. We join his other friends just outside of the city and continue to move on. I am to be the scribe recorder who writes many things down and to be an escort and to listen to everything. To not miss anything. Listen, listen.

NEXT SCENE: FEEDING THE MULTITUDES

C: There's a large crowd. We're handing out fish and bread. He's speaking. He's talking again about nourishment. He's saying to be nourished is to know wholeness, which happens through truly knowing hunger. That in the Kingdom of Heaven, it's impossible to hunger. In this physical dimension, when one knows that there is truly no hunger, then that which nourishes the body appears. The baskets are overflowing. We take a fish; we take a loaf of bread from the top, and it reappears immediately. The hungry are being fed. That is what we are to do to allow our hunger, our yearnings, to collapse and cave in on themselves and carry us to the depth of our awareness. The realization of wholeness, of completeness, of oneness. It permeates every cell out of the molecule; every aspect of mind is in the awareness of every thought, even in playing with the thoughts that involve distinction, division, separation, classification. And to be that which nourishes as a reflection of generous nature to serve.

M: How many would you say are around you?

C: Thousands.

M: What's the mood like there?

C: Gratitude. It's a symphony of gratitude. Praise.

NEXT SCENE: MEETING IN THE GARDEN

C: We're in the gardens a few days before the crucifixion. It's the most famous time when he called out to Judas and was preparing us for what was to come.

M: What's happening there?

C: It's actually very sweet. It's a very sweet moment; it's not so much out of the ordinary. He would often give us little hints about some things that were right around the corner, very playful — even here. So, it's kind of a sense of "Oh, okay, this is going to be coming up," but you know, he's essentially warning us of what he's been talking about. He's been talking about it for a long time. About the true essence of his nature, of our nature, of our preoccupation even with the projection of a physical form. Really inviting us to rewrite our perception of the body as a projection, an extension of consciousness that is not really tied to this life and death cycle as it appears. That is actually the mind, the identification of a servant mind, that is imprisoned — divinely so.

So, he's talking, and this has been one of the things that none of the disciples...this is one of the things that goes over everybody's heads, and they're just like, "I don't know. I don't know really know what you're talking about." And I am connected with that feeling, and I'm also...so he's kind of like playfully leading, "You know what I've been talking about...transformation of life, power, heaven." and now he's saying he's inviting us to, everything that I just said, see through a singular eye (nonduality) to behold the kingdom of heaven on Earth. To look with a singular eye, to be so anchored in nondual awareness and being that we can still engage in a game of polarity where there is a spectrum, where there is what appears to be a Light and a Dark — a positive pole and a negative pole. Dynamic charges. And there appears to be ecstasy and happiness and harmony and safety and also strife and pain and suffering and loss and cruelty.

And that in the space of mastery, in that he is bringing, all the value of all of those experiences are equalized and completely immortalized and integrated. There is no more delineation. He is essentially warning us that the scene is going to be challenging, gruesome, and difficult, but he is speaking of it in a way that it's just another day. It's just anything else. "I'm not going anywhere; nothing is really changing at all. You're still going to be able to feel me; you're still going to be able to hear me like you hear me." We would walk and we could hear him; it's almost like he had a microphone in each of our ears, but really it was he would speak, and we would all hear it in our heads, but it was so audible we thought we were hearing him in our ears.

And so...and then he, the Judas part, he actually asked which one of us is the most willing to... Gosh, what is he saying? He's saying, "the most willing to step into this resonance that I speak of now, the most willing to embrace or surrender or invite that which you would project onto as awful or wrong or bad?" And he steps forward. He is very loyal.

M: You're speaking of Judas?

C: *Yeah. That is not his name. Very sweet, but loyal and a kind person. He had strong convictions. There was a part of him that is almost like he wasn't thinking on as many levels as some of the rest of us, but I think that's that beautiful dichotomy of why some people relate to this. He has a very intricate mind, and other people perhaps think of things more simply, but that doesn't mean that they're not, you know, still in an intelligence vibration. He was a simple man.*

As he steps forward, Master confirms, "Of course it would be you." Of course, it would be you. And so, essentially, what he is saying is you'll know what to do; you must do it; you'll know what to do when it's time to do it; you'll know that it's my blessing.

And that actually this was a lesson for us as disciples because this is what we were to bring into the ministry. It was to embody — conscious divine beings, creators in the flesh. And that was the whole message. The Christ sets you free...the only begotten son...you shall not perish; you will have everlasting life. Everlasting life is the breath of Creation. Creation that we are, that we have at our disposal. This was an initiation into that. I'm getting chills through my whole body; it's the exact same initiation as is happening right now for us in this moment and in the work we are doing to create a space to usher people from prior paradigm enslavement way of thinking into claiming their divine inheritance on Earth — to seeing with that singular eye, to have nondual awareness be dominant. To live as a new human, which is the embodied awareness of the deliberate Creation. To take full responsibility for everything.

The initiation was like 'you are going to see them abusing me.' All this was telepathic; he didn't say all of this, and he didn't say this to Judas. But essentially what he was saying was everyone is going to look at you, and you'll be remembered throughout all of history as being the traitor, as being the one who betrayed, and basically what he is saying is, "You cannot betray me." You cannot betray what we are. You cannot betray the One. That's impossible. Everything that you are seeing, this is an experience, and it's just as valuable and just as beautiful as any other. It's perfect. And I'm not, whatever you think is happening to me because it's happening to this flesh, it's not happening to me, but it's an experience that I get to have through this flesh. And he is speaking of it almost in this fascination way, in that, who is willing to step up and be the one everyone projects their story onto that devalues them as a follower of mine? Well, you need to be the one who is most loyal, right? The most ardent student would be the one that would be willing to take all that, to be seen as the least amongst them.

And so that is why that was him. The rest of us had some measure of doubt; we needed to see more examples — more evidence, more everything. And then most of us were simply grappling with what was left of our humanness, and not knowing how to embark on a life in the time period. It's actually really similar to now, but different.

He said, "Go and tend to my flock." Go and be this ministry; he said it mainly to John and to Mary Magdalene and Peter and some other ones supported, but it was really John and Mary's ministry that they were to take leadership and then all of the other disciples to hold them. He is saying this very rapidly, so everyone was like getting it like, 'What? You are the ministry. You're the magic man.' He's like, 'No, this is this flesh. I live in YOU. This is YOU. This is YOUR Creation.' This is what it is. To go out and do that and still look at the world where it's like...this was when we were following in the glamour of this man performing all these miracles...that was easy, but to embody it in our own consciousness that was still vastly much more limited than him, we couldn't perform all these miracles in the same way. It was daunting. I remember feeling fear, scared, and feeling that he, you know, was kind of being *coy about leaving us. I feel like everyone was kind of feeling that. It's such an interesting thing now.*

In "hindsight" and really to relate to where I am at present to see him looking back at me with knowingness in his eyes and me knowing we could never be apart. Ever. We could never die. We would play together forever. And there is such immense freedom in that, and I can still feel the fear. I can feel the fear in my own body here; how am I going to be this new human?

NEXT SCENE: WALK IN THE GLORY OF MY NAME

C: *I am sitting with the other five on jagged rocks. His body has a glow to it, and it's clear, but not clear at the same time. We all touched it. We felt how solid it is, but also confused. The wounds are still apparent, but not bleeding. This skin glows. He's saying, "Walk in the glory of my name." "Feed my flock, feed my sheep." "Follow my command as it is your command." "Remain the Light and the Truth. Remember always." He's saying that we were lost, but that there will be more suffering and hiding and trials, but he was showing me that this was not so. Suffering is not so. That we each will embody his ministry, the ministry, the truth, in the glorious way. And then he disappeared. The image is gone, and I feel that tingling in my body that I felt when I was a young boy, and he would pick me up. And I feel it coursing through every part of my body. I can feel him touching me from the inside (crying). And I hear him give me a blessing. "March true. There's no law. There is no law."*

M: So, what will you do now?

C: *Leave this country. Leave the Romans. I want to go back to see my mother, but there is no time. There is a commotion, and then I am on a ship bound for Frankia. Someone is there, a soldier with us.*

M: Who all is with you on the ship?

C: *The Priestess (Mary Magdalene), my sister, and three children — his children. Fisherman and ships. And I see the flash with my Light, meditating, writing, and also running and being chased. Being in exile, but also deeply held and thinking much about how the world is crumbling and changing. That there will be a time, a similar time, and it's light and wisdom and memories written down. It will inspire another time, another place, another me. That his name, his beingness that emerges in the flesh as knowing.*

M: How is it there on the ship? What's the mood like on the ship?

C: *Somber. Quiet. Discreet. Sad.*

NEXT SCENE: DYING IN EXILE

C: I'm dying again. I'm older, not too much older — forties. In exile. I had gotten sick, and I'm with the scrolls, parchments, and things that I handed off. And I'm just lying there, just allowing and reading. He comes for me. The angels again, the trumpets, the colors. I allow it to consume me, and there's a flash of light. I'm gone.

M: Will you be returning to your body again?

C: No.

M: This is the end?

C: Yes.

M: What were the last years of your life like? What were you doing then?

C: Different houses in the countryside. Writing, keeping mostly to myself. Had to part ways with Mary and her children as they were taken to even deeper hiding places, disguised. I was caught by the Romans at one point, imprisoned, released, exiled, and then kept watch over. I mostly was quiet and peaceful and writing, and I was able to get some of the scrolls that I wrote to couriers and messengers and people devoted and surrounded around Mary and the kids too. To protect the lineage. Which really is, I told them, ridiculous because he lives in us. He lives in all. Too reactive in the mind, the flesh is not as important as that which animates it. But of course, you can't listen to that. The scrolls were handed to someone in that order. It feels like starvation, or not having food. It's ironic really when the message is so much about nourishment. Remembering when the food was plentiful and even feeling how I am very nourished in my awareness and in my writing. The food in my body was, I think it was the Romans somehow...I think I am in some kind of prison. It's not a traditional prison, but it's some kind of prison. They know where I am, and they control me. They are basically slowly poisoning me. Bad water, stale. Bad bread. My body died.

M: I am wondering if you were the one responsible for writing the book of Revelations? What we call that today in this present time.

C: Much of it. It was, of course, subject to additions and subtractions and other inspired writers. Also, other writers inspired with the human political agenda, but the essence of what I wrote is there. The essence of it is about the coming of a time, the coming of the days of another crumbling of structure. And of the resurgence of the one who knows of his message in the hearts and minds of [inner] knowing too. To usher in the great new era that he was merely a glimpse [of] even a millennia before.

M: When you say the one who knows, who are you speaking of? What are you speaking of?

C: Alpha and Omega. That which is. That which is called parent, father, mother. That which nourishes. That which is nourishment.

NEXT SCENE: THE BOOK OF REVELATIONS

C: I am writing in a stream of consciousness in silence, deliberately. Speak. I have a quill, ink. I intend to use it up, and they are nice enough to continue to give me paper and ink. They, I know that they feel, they laugh because they are going to destroy whatever I write. It doesn't matter. I might as well, but they know that the core of it is going to be sneaked out with this messenger person. Stream of consciousness. A lot of what I read back even to myself didn't quite make sense, but I could feel it's glow. I must admit much of it was beyond me. I didn't even quite comprehend a lot of the specific uses of words, but I know the feeling. The feeling was to claim and proclaim the great cycles and ages and the harmony, how everything fits together and flows in the great dance. By the end, I was at profound peace. There was nothing more to hide from or run from or figure out or know. It was just a profound unfolding and refolding and unfolding and refolding dance.

WORKING WITH THE HIGHER SELF

M: Out of what was shown today, why did you show these certain scenes?

HS: To illustrate the folly of the sense of battle, of loss. To illustrate the perfection and ordered timing to all expression. To convey being reunited, to convey reunion, with that which is. And with this legacy of discipleship, mastery naturally cannot be anything but unfolding perfectly. To remind the personalities of the body, of mind, and you and he and all who perhaps will listen to this voice, your voice, in the coming days to be infused in the sound of truth. To no longer see an adversary for the reflections are surely to come in greater and more powerful seeming form as your voice and this voice and our voice and those other voices infused with the message are to be heard in a greater and greater, more expanded light-sweeping way.

There is to be no adversary, only support, and a dissonance of sound to be invited. To [be] harmony again and for there to be allowed a negative contrasting space that further ignites. It is of utmost importance within your own consciousness, within your own polar energies, and within the mind in every single interaction of that which is seemingly oppositional that it is to be not so.

M: How can we work with that now to embody the truth that there is no adversary?

HS: To not allow the emotion to be projected inward and to follow it to its lowest common denominator, which is an essence of loss, rejection, abandonment, shame, and to allow these deeper emotions to be the master teacher. To be his teaching, a willingness to allow it to break us under the part that is clinging to its identity as less than, as vulnerable, as weak. To be in the living practice of constant annihilation and resurrection, of death and rebirth. To respond with awareness and intention, proactivity, in these moments.

Every single thing and expression is designed to support and encourage the expression and emergence of one's most authentic being. To celebrate in the oneness, the profound opportunity that physical existence is to express the diversity and infinite combination of that one that is, that which is, that which is nourishing. To celebrate in the apparent differences knowing that it is all but fun, you see. Solvent, transient experience. All the play.

M: So, in these times, there are many people that identify as Christian who have been reading and following certain words and languages of how this is going to go during this change. How do we deliver this message? What kind of language do we use that is inclusive to all people?

HS: To court the language as a beloved. To know that it is possible to speak with accuracy, creativity, and clarity. To simplify, to bring words into their most coherent formulation. To be intentional with the motivation behind why you share or speak that which you speak. To be clear in the invitation that it proves, and to whom it is provided unto. To simply remember, is it true? Is it accurate? Is it specific? Does it describe exactly the function of that which I speak, that which I speak into? Is it easily understood and creative? Creative meaning it simply does not piggyback on a concept that is already preconceived or pre-valued. And the ones that do are very intentional in that it is a bridge for something to be familiar enough to simply invite or excite a movement into what is even more accurately describing that which you are speaking into.

FOUR

Mary Magdalene

Mary Magdalene is mostly unknown to the collective human consciousness. The Holy Bible says very little about her. What IS said illustrates a very different perspective of the Mary Magdalene I have come to know through these Quantum Healing sessions.

At the writing of this book, I have worked with three women who have regressed to the lifetime of Mary Magdalene. This is possible as each individual soul is part of a much greater pool of energy called the oversoul. Each client gives their perspective and translation of the scenes as they unfold. What speaks to me in all of these stories is the similarities found in each telling.

In one session, it was too intense for the client to witness the time of the crucifixion because of how traumatic it was for her. I believe that the beings who have been assisting me in writing this book sent me another "Mary" to fill in the missing data of the life of Mary Magdalene. Please enjoy these transcriptions as we explore the life of Mary Magdalene, divine partner of Yeshua ben Joseph.

I met Nikki at a sound healing session I was facilitating at a spiritual center that Ron and I owned called The Lighthouse in Ashland, Oregon. We instantly had a deep connection of the heart that I knew had to be from a past life. For months, I had a nagging feeling that I should reach out to her and ask her if she wanted to do a session. I found her number, called her up, and we found a time to meet up. As I was driving to her home, I had an intuitive feeling that I was going to be getting more of the Mary Magdalene story.

During the interview, Nikki mentioned that she wanted to explore this strong resistance that she had towards Jesus. She had no idea where it came from. She went to church as a young child but never really had any interest in Jesus, just an intense resistance. When I regressed her, she saw herself at the end of an ancient civilization and she was leading many people into a cave system to retreat to Inner Earth and escape the cataclysm and Earth changes that were coming.

When I moved her to the next scene, she started screaming and crying out loud. I was so surprised by the intense emotional explosion and asked her what she was seeing. "They are KILLING MY HUSBAND!" she screamed repeatedly. I tried to calm her down, but she was inconsolable. I received a flash of Christ on the cross in my inner space and asked her to tell me to describe what was happening to her partner. "They are putting him on a cross! Yeshua! My husband!"

At this point, I could not get much information out of her. I asked to speak with her Higher Self. Her Higher Self explained that she carried strong resistance to Jesus because she was still carrying the trauma from witnessing his crucifixion and that she still held resentment towards him for leaving her on the Earth. Her Higher Self shared that I would get more of the story and would work with her about five more times to get the full story.

When I brought Nikki up from trance, she was quite surprised by the whole thing. She had never heard of Mary Magdalene being the wife of Jesus. I asked her not to do any research or speak to anyone about this until we finished the research. This way we could trust that everything that came through would be pure. When I went to send her a copy of the recording, I was shocked to find that the recording did not save. This has happened to me a total of four times and is always during a highly potent session with a powerful storyline. In those moments, I trust that the experience was supposed to be that way, my eyes only, for some reason.

A few weeks later, Nikki and I met for another session. Working with Nikki was a bit of a challenge at times. When she went into trance, her eyes would roll back in their sockets, and she would twitch and jerk as waves of light frequencies rippled through her body. She often responded to my questions with fragmented words. She would slip into deep trance and Mary would incorporate into her channel very clearly and she would speak her inner thought process as Mary out loud. When Mary would run, Nikki's legs would run in place. It was fascinating to watch.

When Nikki came into the first scene, she saw herself as a little girl next to a wooden fence, a horse, and a man who was milking a cow surrounded by straw grass. She wore a black dress and could see her tiny bare feet. When I took her to her home, she saw a building made of long grey stones. When she was eating a meal, she sat with her father and mother.

She described her father as being skinny with dark hair and her mother with orange hair. Her mother was angrily moving about the space serving her and her father food, while her father sat in silence, preoccupied with reading. She said her home felt empty because everyone was always in their heads. It seemed as though her father was always scheming on how to make money to buy food for his family.

The next scene was Mary standing on a great stone pathway outside of what she described as a castle. She was plotting a way to get into the castle, beyond the wall, to try and see her father who had been arrested for stealing. She was considering using her neighbor's horse as a decoy to distract the guards from her real intentions.

NEXT SCENE: MEETING YESHUA

C: *A man speaking. There are so many people around him. He's speaking about God. That God is inside of us. There is Light inside. They're screaming at him. "Blasphemy!" He says the Light...there's Light inside, and that inside connects inside of ourselves. There is power inside of us. He says there is power inside of us. Some people are screaming. What is he saying?*

M: **And how do you feel as you watch them sharing this?**

C: *It sounds funny (laughing). We don't have any powers. We don't have anything (laughing). We barely have food. I can barely survive. The men in the castle, all the guards...it's disgusting what they say. They want us to stay sick and poor so they can be in power. They have all the power. We are being punished...punished. That's why we don't have anything. Don't speak up; don't say anything; hide. Don't dare speak up; don't say a word; hide (whispers)...hide yourself; hide yourself. All our lives...they're small...there is so much, so much...everybody down here is dying...dying...diseases. We don't have any money. We don't have any power. He says we have power (laughs). I wonder, what makes him think that? I'm curious about it (laughing).*

M: **What is it that makes you so curious about this message?**

C: *He looks so well...so well...almost very handsome.*

M: **You think he is handsome?**

C: *(Giggles) Yes. I don't know where he is from.*

M: **Does he share his name?**

C: *Yeshua.*

M: **What is happening now? What do you see happening there now?**

C: *I see a market...and arts...and people giving food, and I have a white basket in my hand...collecting.*

M: How old do you feel here?

C: *Sixteen...seventeen (yawns). People are greeting me; I bow. I see that man again. He's talking again. Healing. Healing sickness. We can heal our own sickness. We can heal our sickness. My mother. His hands, his hands — people are saying his hands; he has healing hands. Healing people with his hands. I wonder if he can heal my mother. I can't...I'm not going to ask. I can't (laughs). I'm so scared...I'm scared.*

M: So, what do you do? What happens next?

C: *"Mary" (very loud voice) ...he says. He must know my name (in a loud voice). "Isn't your mother sick?" I'm trying to hide (whispers). I can't go anywhere. There's nowhere to go. I'm walking backwards. Running. Running...I'm going to get in trouble. I'm going to get in trouble...*

M: Why would you get in trouble?

C: *So scared of these people (body trembling). What if they find out that my mother gets well? They don't like this person (body shaking). First, I'll take care of her.*

M: What are you doing now?

C: *I'm home. Oh, my poor mother. She's got a fever. She doesn't look well. I will have to ask him to come to see if he can help her.*

M: So, you're going to ask that man?

C: *(Nods head yes) Maybe he can come and help her.*

NEXT SCENE: DISBANDING HERETICS

C: *People screaming, people are screaming. The men are coming through their houses. They are looking...looking for that man. They heard he is in this village; he's in this village helping people...telling people that they have power. That there is love, healing, and light and we have to be...and here we are and that's not ok (frantically). That's not ok. We cannot hear this heresy...neighbor's house...is he hiding in the house? (Thrashing and contracting the body like she's running and hiding.) I can't come in here and get in trouble... Oh, my poor mother. I have to help. Lock the door (whispers). "Be quiet." (She becomes very quiet.)*

M: So, you're getting quiet. And what happens?

C: *(Whispers) They're gone.*

M: They're gone now?

C: Yes, gone.

M: So, what do you do?

C: I'm going to go out at night and look for him.

NEXT SCENE: MEETING JESUS AT NIGHT

C: I walk into the forest. It's a bright moon (yawns). I can see the path. It's calm. I have a long coat on to keep me warm and I am walking down a path. It's quiet. Trees. It's very peaceful. I hear a stream. I bend down on my knees and take a drink of the water. (She becomes startled. Body jumps off the bed a little).

M: What happened there?

C: There is a hand on my shoulder. It's him. It's him. His eyes are so blue; his eyes are so blue. He's so strong. I can feel his heart. It's so big and so strong. "Mary" ...he says my name. I'm speechless (laughs).

M: You're speechless? Why is that?

C: (Giggles) My whole body is shaking. I'm sweating. I'm like I know him...I know him.

M: You feel like you know him?

C: Yeah. He's looking at me. He's just staring at me (laughs). "I heard about your hands." (laughing awkwardly)

M: How does he respond?

C: He smiles. I'm blushing. He asks if he can hold my hand.

M: That's nice. Are you going to say yes?

C: Yes.

M: What is it like to hold his hand?

C: Amazing (smiles warmly). Amazing. There is so much power. So much Light. It feels like home. Safe. Warm. Still connecting. He's barefoot in the cold (laughing). We're walking. We're walking down the path towards the village. There is a stone path. We are walking up the stone path. We are looking over the mountains...looking down into the forest and the stars are so bright on this path. Where he is taking me. I don't feel unsafe. I feel very comfortable.

M: So, he's taking you somewhere?

C: Yes, to look at the stars and the moon. It's peaceful and we sit. He asks me if I need help with my mother. (Shaking her head and whispers) "Yes." He says, "You're scared." I'm seeing him watching me. "I asked for your name, and I know I can help you." They took my father and mother. They can do anything.

They don't like him. They were trying to get to him the other day in the village. He's been hiding. Yes.

M: What else do you talk about?

C: How does he heal these people? He tells me I can heal with my hands (starts laughing). That everybody has an inner light, the same as the stars. Open your heart, open your heart and it's all inside of you. No one has more power than the other. Not those men. No one. They can heal with their hands, too. Just believe it. I want to learn more. I want to learn this. "Sit," he says. "Be still and listen." There's a light coming from his heart. It's a shape. Triangles. Always triangles. It's so big and so bright. I feel like the light is filling my body.

M: What's it like?

C: It's so big and perfect. So much love. His hands are on fire. (Her body is shaking, and she sounds as if she is in a state of ecstasy.)

M: What are you experiencing?

C: So much joy and love.

M: What are you two doing there? Describe to me what you are doing?

C: I don't see anything but light. The light is gold. I don't even know where my body is. He let go of my hand (body is now calmer). He is just staring at me. He says pure, pure, pure, so pure. He says that to me. We walk down the hill. Big stones. Big stones.

M: Where are you heading to?

C: This is where he stays. It's stones. One is on the bottom, big one on the top. And there is one on the left and a little opening. He stays in there. He's bringing me inside (laughing).

M: Tell me as it happens what it's like.

C: Just a little cot, a little bed (laughing), a little mattress. And a fire, a small fire. There is nothing else in there. He's sleeping there. He says he meditates in here. He connects the energy from his Father. The sky, the stars, that's where the light comes from.

M: Where does the light come from?

C: Through his body, through his head.

M: Where is it before it goes into his head?

C: From the sky. When he closes his eyes, he sees light, and he feels connected to everything — everything that exists. There is no separation between anyone. Just love. We are one in this body. This body heals itself by connecting to this light. He says I can practice with him. I can practice. Okay. No one knows I am in here. Okay, I can heal my mother (smiles really big).

M: You were saying he talks to his father there. Did he share anything else about his father?

C: His father is not human. His father is in the stars. The vibrations of light and sound.

M: His father is the stars, light, vibration, and sound? Tell me more about that. Did he share anything else about it?

C: This earth has many, many, many stars. There are many stars around the earth. This is one. There are many, many, many stars. We are here to learn.

M: So, he was speaking about one star in particular? And that there are many? Are they all his father or just the one?

C: All of them. One creator of all things. Our Father, all of our Father.

M: Does he share anything about his mother?

C: She has the same name as me (laughter). His mom...was sent the Light. Humans need the Light; she believed in the Light. She wanted to receive it so everyone could feel it and share it with the world. She prayed that the Light would be within her, and that people could see it. She felt it...she felt it come into her body. She saw the gods and goddesses in a circle of light, blue light was actually a circle, and it came into her body.

M: What was that blue light?

C: Yeshua.

M: Where was that blue light before?

C: Pleiades...light beings (body arching and shaking). Vibration...so much vibration. It's so expansive. There is so much Light there. There is so much Light there.

M: What does that mean?

C: Tell me about it. Stars. Stars...lots of love...shining light...they talk to each other through their bodies...their vibration (her mouth was stretching). I have a lot of power (starts gesturing with hands and fingers and making swishing sounds).

M: What gives you this much power? You said you have a lot of power.

C: I feel the power in my heart.

M: What gives you this great power in your heart?

C: Love.

NEXT SCENE: CUDDLING IN THE CAVE

In the next scene, Mary and Jesus are cuddled up inside the cave. She feels Jesus's soft hand in hers while she strokes his hair. She comments on his smooth muscles and giggles. She shared that he tickles her sometimes and whispers in her ears how beautiful he thinks she is. Her smile is beaming from ear to ear as I imagine them wrapped up in one another's arms, staring deeply into one another's eyes, engulfed in teenage love. At this point, Mary is around sixteen or seventeen-years old. Jesus is just a few years older than her. The next scene is with them connecting and playing in Yeshua's cave-dwelling.

M: That's nice. What else do you do with each other when you are in the cave?

C: *We hold each other's Light in our hands. We breathe (camera shows the fingers of both hands being held up) and imagine our bodies all different colors like a rainbow.*

M: So, you fill yourself with this rainbow color? What else do you do?

C: *We create. We create more dynamic energy, and we send it all over. All over...everywhere. We imagine healing, seeing all the people well, food everywhere, and peace. Everyone is taken care of.*

M: That's nice. Does he share where he learned how to do these things?

C: *He says to look in your heart. Relax, be still, and listen to the answers. I feel his chest against my chest.*

M: That's nice. What are you doing there?

C: *Breathing. Breathing in the Light. And we're pulling all the energy up to our chests and filling our hearts. Filling our hearts with more... (she smiles).*

NEXT SCENE: MIRACULOUS HEALING

C: *There is a boat. There are people screaming "that man in the sand!" He's not breathing. He tried to get from the water.*

M: What are you doing there?

C: *I was walking with Yeshua. He runs over and starts to pray...his hands...he starts using his hands. He's praying. I watched him. I saw. This man's face is blue (body shaking and arching). He's praying. There's so much light. (Body still shaking.*

Her hands are up off the bed, fingers outstretched.) The man starts to cough. (She coughs also.) He's not blue. (Still moving her arms and hands and fingers.) And he's fine.

M: A miracle.

C: All the people, they are grabbing him. "Stop grabbing." (Moving her arms and hands rapidly on the bed.) Grabbing his shirt...they're grabbing. They say he can bring back the dead. "Help me, help me." They want help. "How do you do that? I want that. Give me that. Help my mom. Help me! Help my mom!" I'm knocking people down. Everybody is following us. I'm holding his hand. Everybody is following us.

M: What does it feel like?

C: Strange. Powerful. Everybody wants to know who he is. Everybody wants to have him at their house. Everybody wants him. I don't want them to see where we go. Go to the village. Go to the village. I see two horses are racing; we're galloping.

M: Where are you galloping to?

C: Somewhere across the field. We're moving. We're leaving. They want us to go. We want to go. They want us to go.

M: Where will you go?

C: I don't know. They don't understand us. They don't understand us.

WORKING WITH THE HIGHER SELF

M: Thank you very much for sharing what you shared with us today. I was wondering if there is anything you'd like to share about why you shared these scenes. Why did you share these scenes?

C: There is a path to love that creates. I can create, bring life. The universe is so much bigger than we've ever imagined. People want what they don't have. Sometimes they want to take it instead of work for it. They want to stay powerless and broken, and they don't even know how powerful they are.

M: In one of the scenes, Yeshua was explaining that his father is the Creator. I was wondering how that relates to the time that Nikki is speaking of Source, there is also God and also the term Goddess. Can you explain how all of that works together in reference to Yeshua describing his father?

C: The Light co-exists in the level of divine masculine and feminine, equal balance of earth and sky. So, within the Light, there is a masculine and feminine principle.

M: **Can you share some more thoughts about that because I think often people think gods are male, a father. May you share more about the feminine principle of Light, the goddess, the mother?**

C: *The Mother is the purity that gives birth to the physical and holds the Light of all creatures and beings.*

M: **You are saying that the Mother is the purity that gives birth to the physical? So, what is the Father within that?**

C: *The protector.*

NEXT SCENE: LIFE IN EGYPT

C: *Pyramids. Two big pyramids, just lots of sand. A man on a camel who's with us. He's our guide, guiding us. He's dark-skinned, white turban, gown — blue and white. His face is covered, and I can only see his eyes.*

M: **What are you wearing there?**

C: *It's like a blue dress, long cloak, and some sort of thing on my head. It's windy, really windy.*

M: **What's Yeshua wearing?**

C: *White pants and white shirt. We're traveling through. People are growing food. There's civilizations, towns. Something about the towers. These pyramids are towers. There's energy coming from them. It's like this light source; it's really strong. It's a conductor. He's telling us about the water; there's water underneath. It makes electricity, some sort of power. Everybody feels good when these are on. We're here to experience it. It's like the light that comes from the hands, that comes from Yeshua's hands. The healing energy that we use is the same energy. It's a huge, huge resource of healing energy. There are farms; there are lots of different types of farms there. There are aqueducts. Just working on the land. This water goes under the pyramids too. It's creating the energy that's in the pyramids through the tide in the ocean. The river, the rivers, there's rivers moving water, moving energy. Conductor. Conducting.*

NEXT SCENE: PRIESTESSES OF EGYPT

C: *I see lots of women. I see a crowd. Crowds. I see crowns and hooded cloaks. Yeah, there's a lot of women, a council. They're in council. I see a chalice. I see swords. High priestess.*

M: What about the high priestess?

C: Mary. Mary's the teacher. Mary's teaching. Blood mysteries, magic. Sensitivities. Psychic. Getting our moon blood to the earth, earth offerings.

M: What happens when you give your blood to the earth?

C: She receives our blessings. Blessings are received.

M: What happens when she receives those blessings?

C: Peace, healing. Sight. Seeing. (Mumbles) Six stars, six stars, six stars... (Says this about six or seven times.) Six-pointed stars, chalice, six-point stars, moon, sun moon, earth sky, sun moon earth sky, energy, up down, down up, two-directional energy. Ascension, manifestation, Anahata [heart] chakra, divine masculine moving with the feminine. It's multidimensional. When you hold it, you hold it. It connects to the sky. Connects to the earth and it's pulling energy from both directions.

M: How does this six-pointed star become manifest?

C: Through the heart. Focus, we focus on prayer, and it materializes.

M: So, you go into prayer, and it begins to generate from your hands from the Anahata chakra? Then what do you do with it?

C: It's like clear sight. Visions come through it. It's like a crystal. It's so clear.

M: Wonderful. You said you were there with Mary. Tell me more about her. You said she's a high priestess.

C: Mmhmm, she's so beautiful. Light skin, it's like porcelain. Piercing green/blue eyes. So calm. So peaceful. Love, so much love.

M: Wonderful. Are we talking about the mother of Yeshua?

C: Yes. She's teaching all the women. There are thirteen. There are thirteen circles of thirteen. They make the grid. The grid of Light.

M: What happens when these groups of thirteen women meet?

C: We're connecting with the stars. Sirius. Venus. So much Light energy. Clear vision. Clear vision and what to do.

M: So, you know what to do when you get the energy?

C: Organize what to do. How to create things. Plans. Connecting to the stars, the starlight. Helping the people use the earth, the power of the earth. Ascend...ascend; the Earth is ascending. The chakras. Energy, energy centers.

M: Are you talking about the earth centers or the human centers?

C: The human centers and the earth centers. They're both ascending.

M: What does Yeshua do when you're meeting with the women like this?

C: *(Giggles) He supports it. He knows. He's gathering the men. The men protect the land. There are people who are not awake who want to take this land, this sacred land. Men are there to teach and support our plans.*

M: That's nice. So, Yeshua helps to gather the men around to protect and to teach? What kind of things does he teach?

C: *Love, compassion, trying not to fight. Everything is a fight. Teach the feminine. The heart. And to be kind to the land.*

Mary and Jesus are traveling with three boats in what she calls Turkey. They are traveling with three friends named Mark, Anthony, and Simon. They are traveling around trading fish. She describes women on the shore in red gowns and different colored fabrics on display. People recognize Mary, Jesus, and the group and begin to gather and bring their friends to listen. She described a man with armor, who she calls the Prince of Greece, who has come to warn them and tell them to leave the area.

NEXT SCENE: TRAVELING TO TURKEY

M: Why does the prince want you to leave?

C: *Blasphemous, it's blasphemous.*

M: What are you doing that's blasphemous?

C: *Speaking truth: "God is within you." That we have the power inside of us to heal ourselves and to bring peace and love to the people. People have power. People have the power! Power's not in the hands of the few; power's in the hands of many. In everybody's hands. The truth. We teach people. We're trying to teach people. We teach and trade our fish, and we sit and talk. And we tell people of the stars, and we talk about ascension and moving our bodies and healing energy, opening our vision, clear knowing.*

Some hear and some don't listen. Some are so scared; they don't believe it; they don't have anything. They don't have the power to do anything. No rights. We want them to come to our land where there is peace. It's idyllic. There's peace, everyone's fed, and there's lots of love.

M: Where's your land?

C: *Strip of land near the pyramids. So lush. So beautiful. So much abundance. Endless energy. Everybody's needs. They have what they need. We decide to leave. We will return another time.*

NEXT SCENE: STUDENT OF MOTHER MARY

In the next scene, Mary is in a vineyard surrounded by grapevines, red apple trees, and mountains. She referred to the place as Burgundy. She is writing down some of Mother Mary's teachings and plans for creating caring spaces for women to gather. She writes about tantric teachings of divine union between masculine and divine feminine energies which meet together at the heart. She describes notes from her meetings where they would use breath and meditation to create an arc of light through the body similar to the shape of the Egyptian ankh. Later when I brought the client to wakefulness, she was excited because she had never heard of Mary Magdalene doing tantra practices. I encouraged her not to do any research so that we could keep our findings pure.

NEXT SCENE: ANKH OF LIFE

M: How do you use that arc of Light?

C: *It regenerates energy through the bodies. Through the orgasm. You go into sacred soul contact, and you open up your energetic field, and as you breathe together you bring the energy from the root all the way up to the crown and circulate it, bringing it back to into the earth. It activates, it activates sight. The pineal gland. Visions, clear visions. Using it for ascension to understand how to use this human organism to heal the planet.*

M: How else would you use the organism to heal the planet?

C: *Brings down information from the star systems, like an antenna.*

M: How does that work? Tell me what you're seeing there.

C: *It's the Merkaba, the six-pointed star keeps coming up again. (Whispers) Six-pointed star. Torus energy. Spinning, a spinning energy field. The six-pointed star is rotating. It's in the body and around the body, up and down, like a figure eight. It's like a generator. There's limitless energy. It's Creation energy.*

NEXT SCENE: INNER EARTH

The next scene was of Mary descending a staircase inside a crystal cave. It was clear to me that we were visiting a high-frequency space because the client's eyes were fluttering rapidly behind her lids, almost rolled completely back. Her body shuddered as waves of electricity moved through her. It was hard to get much information from her because she mostly spoke in Light language when responding to my questions. I did manage to get her to share that the cavern had white crystalline walls and purple amethyst spikes, shining prisms, and a geode doorway. She was invited down a staircase by tall, pure, white-light energy beings who introduced themselves as Lemurian. She described the environment as pure, loving energy with no suffering at all. I decided to move from the scene once the client descended down the stairs because she would only answer my questions in Light language!

NEXT SCENE: JESUS AND MARY IN JAIL

In the next scene, Mary is inside a prison cell. She and Yeshua had been arrested by a bunch of men and separated into different cells. When I asked her what they did to get arrested, she described them standing amongst many, many people and Yeshua delivering a teaching.

M: What's he talking about?

C: He's talking about love, love and kindness. People are so fascinated by him. He speaks and everybody listens. There's so many people who just follow him around. I see sheep and horses and so many people. It seems like we're always running. We are always running away. We're always hiding and running and hiding and running. I'm so tired.

M: Does it put any stress on your relationship?

C: Yeah. It's hard to find time to be alone, to be intimate. We know that we have plans, but we can never stop. We can't. There's nowhere to stop.

M: Yeah, you just have to keep going, huh? Do you ever fight or bicker?

C: Sometimes, but not that much. Not that much. We understand.

M: Yeah. What do you feel like your biggest challenges are when you're relating, like when you're getting triggered?

C: Just ease, why, why is it hard? It feels like we have to convince people. We feel so much love and they don't feel so much love. Why do we have to convince them of what they have already inside of them? Sometimes it feels lonely.

NEXT SCENE: MOONBLOOD RITUAL

C: I feel walls, stone walls. There's light. It's a tunnel. It's winding around. I'm going to meet the other ladies, the other women. It's a full moon. Rituals.

M: What's the purpose and intention of the rituals?

C: We meet with our blood moon. Blood moons. (moon blood, menstrual blood)

M: You meet with your moon blood? Yes? Why do you do that?

C: It's an offering, offering for the earth. There are thirteen women.

M: What do you do in the ritual?

C: There's six, six women; we stand in a star. We hold our, our blood and a bowl and we pray. We're around an altar. I see a light in the ceiling; it's a hole. It's like moonlight is trying to come through the hole.

M: So, six of you stand around this altar? What do the other women do?

C: They're standing around us. Mother Mary's in the middle. She's the pillar, the center pillar. Pure energy. Every woman has a woman behind her, she's in the center. Each woman holds her blood, and the light comes through from the Moon, and all the women hold their hands up towards the light and the light shines through her crown and she turns into like an angel. She's luminous. So much Light!

M: What are your prayers for in this ritual?

C: Healing, healing the planet. Healing the people.

M: Why do the people on the planet need healing?

C: There's so much greed. So much darkness.

M: So, you're doing this ceremony to help to clear it? How does that work? As you know it you can share. You can see it and describe it to me. What do the ceremonies do?

C: I see triangles of light. It's like a Merkaba. It's like it's three-dimensional. Light emanating everywhere.

M: That's so beautiful. Where are these women from?

C: Different star systems.

M: Different star systems and they're incarnated as a human? Why are they here from other star systems?

C: Yeah. Because the Earth is transcending. The Earth's moving into Light. There are other systems that are, they wanna be on this planet. There's so much life on the planet.

M: So, you've all come to help prepare the planet?

C: There are other beings that are on the planet already. There are beings that come and go from the planet.

M: What do they do when they're coming and going from the planet?

C: The information. There's information here. It's hidden but there are people that are here to access it. Yeshua's here to access it. Nobody wants him here.

M: What do you mean nobody? Who's nobody?

C: The people on the planet. There are forces on the planet that don't want him to be here because he knows how to access it. It opens up the energy fields. It wakes up the people. We're here to protect it. It's underground. There are crystals under the earth. They hold these keys, this information. It's encoded energy. It's under the earth. Crystals. Crystal cities. Just other planets that have encoded it. Stars. Starseeds.

NEXT SCENE: GOING HOME TO THE PLEIADES

The final scenes that I had with Nikki were of her traveling with her daughter Sarah to meet a man from Mt. Carmel who she wished to marry. At this point, Yeshua had already made his Lightbody transformation and would only visit from time to time in Lightbody form or dreamtime to check in on the two of them. There was no mention of other children. When Mary transitioned out of her physical life, she traveled through a tunnel of light to her home planet in the Pleiades. From there she met with her council of guides and described looking out over the multiverse which she described as many "universities" to choose where she was going to incarnate next.

Transcript: Another Perspective of Mary Magdalene

Here is a session with another client who regressed back to the lifetime of Mary Magdalene. Without the clients knowing one another or having any understanding of what material I had, this other Mary Magdalene transmission filled in the blanks where the other client was not able to "see." We can thank the Higher Realms for coordinating that!

SCENE: WITH JESUS ON THE HILL

C: He speaks to the people on the hill. People are sitting and standing and wondering who this man is. Intrigued with his message — some are spies; some are innocents. What does he want with them? How can he change their lives? They are simple people, and they are under the rule of the Romans, so how can he bring them freedom, and yet they gravitate towards his magnetism. What they hear is profound and strange and foreign to them because the rabbis do not speak to them in this way.

M: What does he say to them?

C: He encourages them to be of their own mind and heart. Not to be subservient to any ruling power of the day. That their greatest empowerment is from inside of themselves. They are not lost, yet they keep themselves in that place of being lost, which is why they draw to themselves overlords — because they make themselves out to be victims, and yet they are far from that. He is a rabble-rouser. He is a true rabble-rouser.

M: A true what?

C: Rabble-rouser. He wishes to overturn their hearts and minds as he did the tables in the temple. See the Light. See the Light he implores them. They question because they see one reality and yet they know not of their Creator-given abilities to become more than they are. They...they talk amongst themselves. They question. They question him. They question themselves. Some are quiet and pensive. They realize what he says with his stories and his words, it makes sense — yet, what are they to make of this? They hear stories; they have seen his miracles, and so there is a part of them that wants to believe, and they feel his magnetism which is...and his love, genuine love.

And so, this is why they, they follow in a way, they want to hear more. It's like putting one toe in the water, and then another, and then the foot, then the ankle — slowly, slowly dipping in to find out more because they are curious even though this is strange. And even though, they wonder about him and who he is. He implores them to search their hearts and minds for meaning and purpose — greater than the reality they are existing in now. Something greater. Something more magical. Something more empowering.

M: Well, what do you do as he gives his message? What are you doing there?

C: I am listening. I follow. Some women — some people — mostly the women, the men do not really engage. The women — they have questions, and I do my best to respond in the way that I can from what I have understood of his teachings.

NEXT SCENE: THE LAST SUPPER

C: It's the Last Supper. Passover. And the disciples and some women around the table. There is wine; there are flatbreads. There is a lot of talk and a lot of jovialities.

M: What happens next?

C: Yeshua looks across at Judas. Judas looks at Yeshua. They stare into each other's eyes. Judas almost shakes his head as he can't do this. He cannot do this (whispers), and Yeshua looks into his...directly at him, and it is like they are transfixed. "You can do this," he says to him. "And you will. You will follow the will that has been declared in Heaven. Will you not?" They are locked into some invisible transmission. He stands up — Judas — and he is angry. He is very angry and afraid at the same time. He pushes his chair so violently that suddenly there is silence. Everyone looks around. "What is the meaning of this? What is the meaning of this," they ask? He looks at Yeshua one last time, and Yeshua is resolute and calm at the same time. He has a great knowing in his presence — a sadness, a knowing. And Judas leaves the room.

Everyone is quiet, quiet. What is going on? They start to ask Yeshua, "What is going on? What is happening?" He is silent for a few minutes. It seems like an eternity. "I will not be with you for long," he says. "Not in the way that you have known me to be." Suddenly there is shouting. "What, what, what do you mean? What is this? What is happening?" He raises his hands. "Stop. Bring your peace, bring your hearts to a place of peace and trust in the will of the Heavens. Trust in the name of Hashem. This is not what I have taught you. This is not what I have taught you."

I am feeling a little shocked and dismayed, and I observe the men. They are confused, reactionary. They look over at me, some of them, and I have nothing to offer them but just my silence. They think of themselves. "What are we to do? What's to become of us?" they ask. "Greater things you will be and do than I have," he says. "I have taught you well. You will spread the message. You will go out and teach amongst those who have ears to hear and eyes to see who you are and what you are about. Do not despair. I am with you always. I am in your heart of hearts. I will always be with you. And so, you will carry out that which you have been ordained to, and fear not, I am with you always. Your steps will be guided. Your thoughts will be directed. And you will journey amongst mankind and spread the message of love, and this is all I can say right now. Follow your hearts and believe in your message of love — all that you have seen and heard and learned. Remember these words, and we will go now. It is time to let what needs to unfold. Let it happen."

SCENE: THE CRUCIFIXION DECISION

C: *Chaos in the streets. There is chaos in the streets. He has been taken. He has gone in front of Pontius Pilate, and we know not where he is exactly. And the disciples are in chaos. "How could this be? Such a great man. How can this be?" They are in denial. Many times, they are in denial. Some flee. They hide for their lives. Some are standing in the shadows observing. There is commotion amongst the people in the neighborhood. They don't like to have the presence of more soldiers than is necessary — especially this night of Passover. Consternation. Fear. Deep fear. Everyone is unsettled, and most stay awake through the night. Incredulous. In deep denial. Confused.*

And Judas is kneeling. There are no words to describe his sense of...on the one hand, it's betrayal, and yet, on the other hand, he was gifted with a vision from Yeshua for this higher purpose. But how can he live with himself? The physical wounding is too deep. He goes away. He dares not show himself in front of the others, for he knows they will kill him. So intense is their anger and sense of betrayal. So much commotion. Questioning. I have hope, and yet, my heart pounds. I cannot leave this place until I know what it is to be.

The darkness turns to light. The sun is coming up, and we are still waiting for news of him. Still hours away. My gut aches. My heart aches. I need to be with the children, but I need to be here to know where he is and what will be. I run to them to comfort them. There is someone to look after them until I find out what is going on. My heart races. I race back. Together with Mother Mary, we are holding each other. We support each other.

M: What happens next?

C: *There are rumors that he is to be held for a little while the courts decide. My head is hurting. It's...I am filled with fatigue, and the hours are long, but eventually, they have decided that he will be crucified. There is great shock and disbelief. "How can this be? How can we, how can we save him?" The women cloister around Mother Mary and me (deep breath). They offer love. They offer support. My knees are weak, and I feel like buckling down to the earth. Weak. I have to see him. I have to see him. But still long hours before (pauses) anything* happens. This is excruciating pain, and my body is numb. I cannot eat. The women force us to drink water. Stay hydrated. But I cannot eat anything. The men have fled. Although I hear some are hiding close by.

And then there is news they will bring him out. It is to happen that day. And it will happen in a hurry because of Shabbat, and the Sanhedrin have declared it needs to happen before Shabbat. Who are these people who are so blind to the truth and what he has tried to do? His message of love goes above their heads. They have the power, and they fear him. They fear the crowds and the miracles he has drawn and performed. Want him gone. They want him out of the way. He is interfering with their relationship with the Romans — the status quo. Who are the traitors here? Who are the traitors here? Then the gates open and there is a great uproar. People running and calling out, and I see him. Finally, I see him! Oh, my Lord. Hold on!

M: What is it like to see him?

C: They have pushed the thorns into his crown into his forehead. He is bleeding over his face. Mary and I and the other women...we...they are supporting us to stand. It is so hard for me. I cannot endure this vision of him. I cannot be...one of the soldiers walks behind him with a whip (gasps)...and they position him to a cross. They tie his wrists to the poles. He buckles, but they pull him up, and they command him to walk. And people...so cruel. Some are jeering; some are crying; some are just watching. The Roman soldiers are pushing them aside as he walks through. "Raboni, Raboni — look at me. Look at me. Please look at me." But his eyes are...he walks and yet his eyes are...I feel he does not see us. He does not see me. The wood makes a trail in the sand. As it goes over the stones, it makes that noise of being dragged along. It's too much to bear. I cannot...I cannot. (Big breath.) It's too much for me. We follow. Just crying in disbelief. How can this be? How can he endure this? How can this be? We see Joseph of Arimathea. He comes running over. He is speaking to Jesus, Yeshua. He is saying prayers in Aramaic. Walking...it is too long out to that place. They have prepared two others on either side. They are already there; it is agonizing to see them up. I have never wanted to see this, and now I am faced with it with my beloved.

I say prayers for him. I implore Hashem to give grace to somehow change this all — somehow stop this madness — this insanity. I feel my pleas and cries are not being heard because everything is going as they wish it to. They are nailing him — his palms — and tying his feet to the bottom. I cannot bear this. I cannot. My head feels like it is going to explode. We are weeping and weeping *and weeping. We are being held by the other women — Elizabeth, Joanna, Ruth. They torture him so. He is bleeding. His body is filled with blood. And we sit at his feet below him. Weeping, crying for each other, for him, for his torture — for this pain, for this agony. They want to hurry this up because Shabbat is coming. The Roman pierces his side — ahhh. His body writhes in pain, and the blood spurts. It is too much. It is too much.*

He telepathically says to me, "My love for you is...is eternal. We are always together. We will always be together." The people start leaving to go home for Shabbat. I want to stay. I cannot leave him. They have taken him for dead, but I feel there is still life there. I feel there is still breath in him. He is not gone. He has been trained. He has been trained in the East. He knows how to hold that energy force despite everything that is going on in his body; he's holding on. He was trained for this. He was trained to hold his soul despite the condition of the body. I know he can do it, and he will. Just holding on. They have decided to bring him down. Joseph helps to unbind his wrists and feet. Oh...the nails. I can't bear it. I cannot bear to look as they release him from the...cross. Joseph is crying. He loves Yeshua as his son. He weeps as he cleans him. I hear "All is not lost. He is here. He is still with us." My body is weak from the trauma. Mother Mary and I, we hold each other. And before I go, I want to clean his body too. I want to wipe his body, so he is clean. So, I help Joseph. They wrap him up in the liniments and place him on a cloth that they can carry. They take him away to the tomb. I have to go home. It's Shabbat. I have to see my children. My love, I will see you. We will be together. I know. I know we will. I will see you. I will see you, and we will be together. (Deep breath and sigh.) We have to go.

M: Tell me what happens next.

C: We are up all night. I cannot sleep. I am just rocking and rocking and rocking. Just Mary and me and some of the other women. I need to find faith and trust that this is what the Divine Spirit wants. What he agreed to. What he came for...and perhaps it could have been different.

M: What did he come for?

C: To wake people up. To overturn their consciousness. To bring them to love — back to love.

M: So, what happens next?

C: Shabbat is long. I want to go back to the tomb.

M: Go back to the tomb.

C: It's empty. The tomb is empty. Where is he? Where is he? Where are you? Where are you? I am standing outside. I don't know where he is.

NEXT SCENE: PARTING WORDS

C: He is there with the disciples, and he keeps his distance from them. He has to tell them what their mission is. He has to inform them that he cannot be with them in the physical as he will go away. It is not safe for them to be together. And it is their choice — those that wish to travel to spread the message as far and wide as they can and to leave as quickly as they can because it is not safe; they will be hunted down. It is a dangerous time. They have everything they need. They will always be provided for. They must go forth. His energy, his illumination, is inside of them, and that divine spark will be the words that come from their mouths — be the thoughts that they think — that guides them to be where they need to be, to journey in the directions they need to go. They are always guided and protected when they listen to that inner guidance.

Some will not escape the wrath of the overarching powers of the day, and it will be their destiny to fulfill this further will of their soul contract. Everything in life is as it is meant to be. Have faith, trust, be strong. This is why they came to Earth at this time with him. They have the energy and the love in their hearts to be that guiding light, to be that teacher, to be that healer for others who are ready to hear the message. He must go. I must go. I will be taken with the children and my maidservant, and we will go with Joseph of Arimathea. We must leave in a hurry. There is no delay. There is no time to tarry. We need to leave. Some of the men cry like children. They weep for their master. And yet they know this is the hour for them to step out into the world and be strong and be brave. So, they disperse.

Yeshua and I stand in front of each other. Our eyes are locked in that now, that knowingness, love. "Everything will be fine," he says to me. "Joseph will take care of you. You will all be fine, and I will be fine. I need to go away. We all need to go away. What has transpired is...is what is meant to be. You will, in your own right, be that love in the world. You will bring the children up with that love as only you know how. And you will find community, and you will find solace in the love that you receive as much as you share."

M: Does he share with you where he's going to go?

C: He will return to the East to his teachers there. He will return to the monastery that he stayed in when he was younger. Perhaps he will live out his life there. Perhaps he will return. He does not know. For now, he needs to journey east, and I will go west. To "fly on the wings of Spirit," he says to me. "Fly over the water; be safe. Be sure. Know my love is with you always. I am inside your heart as

you are in mine. And not a day will go by that I do not think of you and bless
you and send you my love, as I know you will for me."

SPEAKING WITH THE HIGHER SELF

M: And in the lifetime with Mary, why did you show the scenes that
you showed?

HS: Her presence, her presence as a grounded, holding energy — she could hold
the space for Yeshua. She could match the complementary energies in a receptive
way — the magnetic, empowered, receiving, holding, sharing a balanced way.
And she did this for him. It has taken many lifetimes to build her vessel to be
that, and she did. She was his grounding while he traveled and spent most time
in Spirit. She was grounded in holding that space for him.

M: We were wondering — Jesus the ministry was brought to the
collective at that time, and the collective was in a certain
vibration in a certain way — we were wondering how that
message translates to this time? What is needed in this time for
the collective?

HS: The codes — the love, the energy, the consciousness was implanted and
imprinted into a deeper matrix on the planet at that time to be unearthed as
such, revealed in this time for the collective — for humankind. And so, it has
lain dormant, overlaid by the false matrix that was input through control and
narrative on the planet. It was and is emerging now more and more as the
collective awakens. The message of love, beauty, truth, joy, play, empowerment
— the ability to create this new reality, this new creation, and birth this new
light on the earth. It was an imprint into the collective unconscious at that time,
and that imprint in the unconscious is being triggered as and when each of the
seven-plus billion souls are ready to awaken to it.

M: When I share this type of information publicly — there are
people that consider themselves devout Christians who say
things to me like I am being led astray by the darkness or by Satan
because I don't stick to the narrative that they learned in church.
What's your perspective on that and how to respond to it?

HS: Well, we know those projections are projections from people's own shadow self,
their insecurities, their inability to transcend the boxes they have put into their
minds. They will point fingers because they do not know anything else, and it
is safe to do that; it gives them power over their insecurities. They do not wish

to rock their own worlds, their little bubbles, because they would not know how to experience anything different at this time. So, therefore, they project at you. They do not know how to handle your truth, your knowing, your innate wisdom. There is no response to people until they do their own shadow work, until they drop their consciousness into their heart. It is only when they live from their heart that they can access the truth — see it, feel it, sense it, know it, hear it.

The only way is to love them and leave them. Send them love. That love, that light, into their hearts and into their energy field is what will impulse them to go deep and deeper into their unconscious. They will open access for the light to heal the shadow — to bring the shadow into the light. They have been trained in something that was falsified for greater purposes of another agenda, and so one can only feel compassion for them at this time.

M: Yeah. So, what is the next stage of that work that the ministry started at that time? What is our next stage of that?

HS: As more of the collective wake, and as the valuable work that you do supports people to understand and clear their core issues, more and more people will come to that place of deeper inner knowing and trusting of the truth that is unfolding on the planet at this time. It happens one person at a time. On a quantum level, it is expeditiously ramping up —mMore so than we can even imagine. And so, that inner truth that has been with us always and is innate to us all — every single soul on this planet — will be birthed with each soul opening in its appointed time, for its appointed reason. And they will, we will, humankind will collectively be transported into the matching vibration of that energy — the ascension of consciousness.

M: Thank you. If Jesus were alive today, what would he share with us to inspire our awakening?

HS: It is very simple. Know that ye are love. He would teach. He would lead by example to be love. It is all energy; it's all vibration; and he would be in the marketplaces; he would be in the fields; he would be in the cities; and he would just be — that love that is highly magnetic. His presence would open hearts, and people would be inspired to seek the truth, and he would encourage them to go inside and find the truth inside of themselves and to themselves live their presence, which is the highest form of love they can be. And they, in turn, would spread that energy and so it would go around the entire planet. And that way...very simple yet we have overcomplicated our lives. And he would overturn much of the teachings of the church. He would invite people to discard all they would deem as the higher ruling authority. He would empower people to be their own leader in love and truth. You do not need emissaries. They are their own emissary to their true light and creative source.

M: I learned growing up, the quote that was used often was from Jesus saying I am the Light and the Way and the Truth. What does that mean? What did that mean from him?

HS: The energies, the codes of love, the sacred geometry, the light that is, and at that time was his energy field — the DNA. It's all energy. This is the energy that will open up. This is the connecting bridge for people to connect into their own hearts to find that consciousness, that super consciousness — unify all that is inside. He was carrying...he was the consciousness that is emerging on the planet today. That consciousness is the build, the bridge builder; it is the wayshower, so therefore he is the wayshower. His consciousness is the wayshower to each person's empowerment, to each person's revelation of their own personal light and ability to transcend and ascend into the highest realms that they are ready for. I am the Way. He is the bridge. His energy field is the bridge. His consciousness is the bridge. It is not about the physical avatar per se as it is the recording of the DNA that he in-filled and imprinted into the subconscious, and that's what needs to be revealed and aligned with the superconscious and conscious aspects of self. Yes.

M: Aha. What was the greater purpose and intention of his life at that time, and what did he leave behind for us?

HS: The culture at the time and society was lost and in decay. It was losing itself in circumstances that were drawing people away from their greater sense of self and purpose and community and sharing. There was an indulgence in material, the material world, and so, there was a split between the spirit and the material. He came as that bridge builder to draw people back into their hearts, connect to their spirit to take back the sovereignty of their essence — soul essence. The soul is sovereign and was being buried deeper and deeper into the psyche and the unconscious. It was his mission to bring the revelation of the soul back to the conscious heart-minds of the people to find balance, to find personal freedom. And finding their empowerment at that time, they would have overcome the need for the oppressors as the mirror to their victim mentality. And in this time, he will say the same thing again. To overthrow that victim mentality, and in doing so, you eliminate the need for the oppressors to weigh down on humankind.

We are no longer slaves. We never were. It is time to shed the shackles. It is time to free the mind and the heart. It is time to find the soul buried deep in the unconscious and bring her up to her former glory — to seat her in her throne of love in the heart and to relegate the ego to be seated behind the throne as the humble servant. The ego, whilst needed in some way, shape, or form, usurped the beauty of the soul, and now she will regain her rightful place. And the ego will be the servant and do the bidding of the soul as was always meant to be. And this is part of the transition, part of the emergence, part of the ascension, part of the revelation.

M: Some people say that his flipping of the tables was a justification of anger in some ways. Why did he flip those tables?

HS: Righteous indignation. Spiritual righteousness. In overturning the tables and causing the money to fall to the ground, it was a symbolic, metaphoric gesture to place the material on the earth. To turn the table upside down was to reveal the vessel — an empty vessel — meaning the vessels of the people were empty, devoid of any connection to soul and Spirit. The vessel being the empty table overturned, sat on top of the money — meaning — build the vessel, infill it with light and love as the true meaning of life. And that the earth and whatever the earth can provide comes secondary, or comes naturally, abundantly, automatically, and with grace through the love of that vessel, filled with light and joy and creativity, and putting that intention into life.

The legs of the table turned upwards are symbolic of the arms of the human raising up, reaching up to the heavens, the Light, to Source, to Spirit to infill and build the vessel with Light and Love. The flat surface of the table like the avatar — when upright blocking the infusing light, but when turned over and lying flat on the ground, covering the money — the material being secondary to the Light; the arms are reaching up to the Light to receive the Light into the empty vessel.

MESSAGE TO HUMANKIND FROM HIGHER SELF

We have shifted to a new realm as more of the collective wakes up. The healing is starting to infiltrate deep into the unconscious psyche to release the fear that was placed upon humanity around this particular event. The debris is being cleansed and cleared and will continue for some time throughout the collective as that old matrix is falling away, that old paradigm of control.

The message is to record, re-envision the new reality that is being birthed. Live it, feel it, sense it, taste it, smell it. It is to be your ongoing experience in the new lives being birthed. A new you is emerging, and we speak to the collective. You can put away those old stories. They no longer have any — should no longer have any emotional charge. They are being cleansed out of your emotional subconscious, unconscious energy fields. You are being cleared of all of that drama that was perpetrated to keep humans enslaved. Do you know this now? Will you awaken to this truth and believe it and then release it without any judgment — only love in your hearts — for the storyline that kept you enslaved just as long as you needed. And as you give up your victim role, so more and more truth will be disclosed, and more and more of the perpetrators of that lie and deceit will come to reveal themselves or be revealed.

And we ask that you see the bigger picture for both the Light and the Dark on the planet and find forgiveness in your heart as every single person in the collective has had some part to play in the dance between the light and the dark. So, therefore, we can release this polarity and the game of the polarity and the story of the polarities through the love that we share in our hearts. Release any emotional charge; release any anger; release any fear that no longer serves the collective or any individual. The story, the narration is now passed, and we ask you to recognize this. It is no longer relevant in this new reality and the birthing of this new Earth. There is no place for any of this in Heaven on Earth. Enjoy your freedom. Enjoy your freedom; enjoy your empowerment. Enjoy the All That Is. Enjoy the moment of your creative expression and how you can infill this beautiful planet, bring her back into harmony and stasis through all the elements and all the four directions.

As we all work together now to heal and clear, release and transform, and enjoy the beauty, the reality that is — the Earth that she was meant to be and will be soon.

Dropping the Veils, Rising in Love

Let us move beyond the illusions of separation and come into deep unity with our own Inner Christ. Let us use the redemptive power of forgiveness and compassion to stand in our divine-human expression and be ambassadors of eternal grace and eternal love.

Let us be visionaries of Paradise upon the Earth and walk forward into this new light spectrum reality and build a New Earth.

FIVE

Jeremiah: Disciple of Jesus

When Dina came into the scene, she described big cumulus clouds and a jade-colored sea. The landscape was dry, and she stood on a pier or dock. When she looked at her body in the scene, she described a bald man wearing a red and blue tunic with sandals. He is carrying a satchel of sacred texts containing the teachings of Jesus and a shepherd's stick, a crook. The man has a wife and a son and lives in a simple home.

SCENE: HEALING MIRACLE

C: *I'm at a fountain. There's a gathering. There's a teaching today. Everyone's really excited. I think...Jesus and his disciples are coming. He's going to be performing a healing. There's a blind girl, and she's going to see again...or see...or see for the first... Well, there are people there that believe and lots of people who don't. It's a dangerous time to be doing healing.*

M: **What makes it so dangerous?**

C: *People are unhappy about his teaching and the people who are following him...who know the truth of his words. I'm there because there's something wrong with my son. He can't walk. Yeah. My son and I are sitting by the fountain. Hopeful.*

M: **Do you have a name for your son?** (C: *Daniel*) **What do you call yourself?** (C: *Jeremiah*) **What's happening now, Jeremiah?**

C: *I'm taking my son through the crowds to Jesus and asking for help, for healing. I'm nervous. I'm elated and happy. He's wearing creamy white...creamy clothes...long robes. Dark hair. Dark skin. He's beautiful. He's welcoming me, asking me what it is I've come for. He knows that I believe and that I've been passing along his teachings to my friends and family. I've met him before. We're watching him heal the little girl. It's powerful. He has his hands over her eyes, and he's speaking in Hebrew. It's like the light in the courtyard has gotten brighter. Everything feels electrified. There are people crying in joy and awe. And...now he's done, and she's laying there, and he asks her to open her eyes. She's crying. She can see. And he's looking at me...and I'm bringing my son to him... I'm asking for healing, but it's difficult. It feels like a burden to ask when he's already given me so much, so much wisdom...but it's not for me, it's for Daniel. And he smiles and laughs. He has a good laugh. And he holds my boy in his arms. (Deep exhalation)*

M: So, he's holding Daniel in his arms now? What's happening?

C: Well, Daniel looks happy...but he's supposed to be this way. He's not going to walk. And I feel sad and...that there's a different path for Daniel. Not one that he needs his legs. That he needs his mind so he can be a great channel...a wealth of information. He's here to observe, and he is very...he's to use his craft.

M: So, he has a different path. How does that feel?

C: Conflicting. But I know that...in my soul that it's true, and I feel at peace with that. I want to...I ask if I can follow him...if I can travel with him. He leaves it up to me. He says, "If you would like. Yes." I decide to go. Even though I feel sadness because I want to be with my family and provide for them, I feel a calling to walk.

M: Does he deliver a teaching that day?

C: Yes. He's teaching about love and what separates us from love and from being connected and how...no matter who we are or where we come from or what journey led us to this place now, we're all the same. We're all one. Your beliefs don't necessarily have to all be the same as long as you're living in your highest self and sharing the joy in your heart with others. You forgive. (Deep exhalation) In a lot of ways...teaching that it's not about religion and the rules and asking us to lay down our swords against each other and to join hands in harmony. Teaching us that each of us is divine. And...talking to the people who are gathered in the back who are angry that he is there and telling them that he loves them and that it isn't magic or heresy or...it's God's Light and Love that moves through him.

M: And how do they respond?

C: Some of them are scared because the girl can see. And some are angry, and some are crying because they witnessed a miracle, and they can't explain it.

M: And how does he handle it?

C: He's smiling. He's just loving them.

M: Is it just him, or did others come with him?

C: No. Others are there. There's a woman.

M: A woman? What is she doing?

C: She's standing...a little to his left, a little bit farther back, behind some of the men, but she's important.

M: How can you tell she's important?

C: There's just a presence. There's a connection. It's like she's standing behind out of respect, out of tradition, but she is close to Jesus. Yeshua. Not Jesus...it's the wrong name.

M: What else do you notice about the group that came with him?

C: They're all so peaceful...except...one of them is still learning...still...I can see him clearly. He has a beard and a gruff, harder face. He had a different name. His...name was Saul. Now it's Paul.

M: Mmhmm. What else do you notice about Paul?

C: He's still at the point where miracles of Yeshua are overwhelming in a way. It's a lot for him. It's awe-inspiring. It's letting go of past beliefs and stepping forward into true understanding.

M: Mmhmm. What else do you notice as you look around at the group?

C: Everyone is hard traveled. They've been traveling a long way. They're tired, but also there's a light about them. It's comforting to be in their presence, but they've come a long way to be here.

SCENE: RESURRECTION TEACHINGS

C: (Deep exhalation) We're inside. It's dark. It's a tunnel. And torches light the way. It's a very sacred place. My body feels very hot right now.

M: What's happening in the sacred place? What are you doing there?

C: We're...learning ancient alchemies of life and death, and there's a blue fire.

M: A blue fire? Tell me about this blue fire and what you're learning there.

C: (Deep exhalation) I want to say we're learning how to raise the dead...to bring someone back to life...something...I don't know.

M: Well, relax into it. Allow more information to emerge. You're going to be raising something from the dead?

C: Yes. This is...we're learning. We don't know how yet, and so today is the day we move from smaller to a larger animal. And Yeshua's not here; he's in the flames. You see his face in the flames, and it's like he's whispering through the fire to us.

M: What is he whispering to you?

C: He is saying that only God...the true power of God can bring someone, something back and only in very certain circumstances...this is a sacred place where only very few people will go in order to learn. The fire is getting bigger because we are bringing back this little calf, and it's making my head hurt.

M: So, you're bringing back a small calf? How do you all do it?

C: It's a laying of hands and words from a book...a book lost to us now.

M: If it's appropriate, you can share the words with me.

C: (Deep breath) From ashes, we come and ashes we rise, as you lay dying, you lay ascending... (long pause).

M: What's happening now?

C: We're all joining hands around the fire, and the calf is on an altar and starting to twitch and move. Energy...that energy is so strong in the room. It's very powerful and very...it's almost frightening, but not in a scary way...but in a scary, powerful way. The calf is walking around (chuckles).

M: That's wonderful. Who are the other beings that are with you? Look around and describe who's with you.

C: There's a woman. There are actually three women. And...two men. One of them...I think...well, she has a headdress on... You can see her face. Black-brown hair. A plain dress. The other one is older. Very old and very wise. She seems to be the teacher of the younger one I just described. I think they're related.

M: What about the other woman?

C: Um...she has blue eyes and blonde...no...light brown hair. She's different. She's not from here.

M: What do you mean she's not from here?

C: I don't know. She's not like everyone else. She's very like...she has more...she has lighter skin...and fair. Not from this part of the world or...maybe not even of this world.

M: Mmhmm. What about the men? What do you notice about the men?

C: They're very holy men. They're quiet. Tall. Funny hats on. Um...but expensive, very expensive robes. They're like high up in the church...I don't know if it's called that...but important figures.

NEXT SCENE: GROWING UNREST

C: We're riding. Hmm. There are palms. People have palms. Following...um...a procession...on our way to a council on something...I don't know.

M: What will you be meeting with them about?

C: There's great unrest. The people in power don't like the teachings of Yeshua and the things we have been learning and sharing with...with the public and with...with each other and...it's...but the people, the people are so thrilled and happy to see him. So, it's very conflicting sides and voices.

M: What's happening now?

C: We're entering into a tent, and I'm in the back. I'm not important...not that I'm not important, but I'm not in the main circle.

M: What's being discussed there? What's happening?

C: People are asking Yeshua to...to just take a break for a minute and let things settle down. They're worried. They are advising...they're advising him to...I think to go into hiding. But he doesn't want to. He's very determined to push forward...to continue with his work...and...

M: What happens next?

C: I don't know. I'm scared. I'm scared for him. I don't... He's my friend, and I don't want anything to happen to him. I think it's more...it's beyond my...my human understanding of what's happening. He's...he says it's time to do the washing of the feet, and so...because we've been traveling a long way. So, we're washing each other's feet, and there's great joy in this. It's a very intimate connection between everyone in the room. And, um, a woman is washing Yeshua's feet, and they know each other. He seems to have a great connection to her.

M: What do you notice about their connection?

C: I want to say it's Mary Magdalene.

NEXT SCENE: TAKING JESUS AWAY

C: I'm so sad (emotional). They're taking him away, and we're in hiding...or I am. They're...I'm devastated. I'm...my teacher and my friend is going to die, and I'm scared because I put down everything to follow him and I don't know...what I will do or [how to] move forward...it's confusing. It's like I know that everything is okay, but at the same time, I have a great fear of what's to come. I'm not hiding. I've come out of hiding, and I'm in the crowd, and I'm watching. It's horrible.

M: What's happening now?

C: They beat him. And he's bleeding, and they're walking him over...(emotional). They're walking him over to a cross and making him carry it. I want to yell out, and I want...(emotional) to tell him that I'm there, but it doesn't matter.

My heart aches. We're watching him walk up the hill...and...there are many of us gathered. There are many that have hate in their hearts for him, and those of us who don't are quiet. Trying to support from afar and...(exhales). Then... They're nailing him to the cross. He's screaming (emotional). It's so painful to watch, and some people are laughing. I want to leave, but I stay...and...I'm trying to force my way through the crowd (exhales). I make it to the front and I'm trying to fight the guards and...I did what he didn't want me to do. I let my emotions take over. This is...I'm getting arrested and beaten and...I'm so angry that this is happening to... It's like all the lessons I learned and the teachings, they went away, and I let my love and my fear take over (deep exhale). I think they kill me. I think...I don't see anything else.

Transcript: Resurrecting a Dead Calf

Here is a transcript from a client named Tyra. I worked with Tyra several months before the client above. I never know where my clients are going to go or what they are going to run into during the session. The energies during this session were so powerful that my client was shaking back and forth as her system was being upgraded. You can imagine my surprise as she seemingly described the previous resurrection process as mentioned before.

C: *It's a temple. It looks like a temple from India maybe. It's a temple. A place of worship and study. The floors. They look like marble. Wow... it's very expansive inside the temple. The floors are white marble with black veins, and I have sandals on my feet. I think I'm female. I'm stunning! I'm otherworldly beautiful.*

M: What are you wearing?

C: *It's like a gown. It's funny because it seems Egyptian, even though the temple seems kind of like India, but I feel Egyptian in the way that I look. It's white shimmery with an inch-wide gold edging. It looks very Egyptian. I think I have a staff. Just a staff, I don't know why...it implies leadership. It implies this sort of status. It feels powerful in a way. I don't know if it's literal, but I feel like I could clap it onto the marble and command things — attention, change, something to materialize even. But I'm not entirely sure if that's metaphorical or true, but that's the feeling of the staff. I'm going to set it down, okay? So, I can pay more attention to myself for a moment. I have a headdress on too. It's very Egyptian...maybe I've traveled.*

M: What does the headdress look like?

C: *It's gold. It's simple but has a stone at the center of it. It sits above my head. Wow!*

M: **What's the headdress for?**

C: *It's again like status.*

M: **Do you live in this place?**

C: *I think I'm teaching here.*

M: **What are you teaching?**

C: *Oh! How to move matter. Yes. You have to command the matter. You can command the matter to change, to move, to use your will. To use your will joined with Creator's will. I see many things moving around in the air, around me. Mmm. I am very serious in a way, although things keep striking me funny, too. I'm a good teacher.*

NEXT SCENE: BLUE FIRE AND THE BREATH OF GOD

C: *We're in a room that's dark. It is dark on purpose. There are no windows; it's an inner sanctum. It has a blue fire. There are others. Yeshua is here. This is a very sacred gathering. It's very holy. We're in the holy of holies.*

M: **What's happening in this gathering?**

C: *It's like learning to raise the dead, animate life. We are learning to breathe this holy fire...we are breathing the breath of God. And we are joined as one mind and one heart and one purpose. We're like a sacred gem, like a sacred sapphire. We're animating life.*

M: **What are you animating now? What do you see?**

C: *I see a calf. The calf had died and we're bringing it back to life. It's a joining. It's a oneness of our energy. We became one, fused, with intent, and we've pulled down the Breath of God.*

M: **How do you pull down the Breath of God?**

C: *You will it to be so. You come together in pure intent. We're there for one reason. One reason only — that is to understand the Will of God. Operate as one with the will of All That Is. We join in the Fire of Light. It's blue. It's the first sign that you've joined as One. Sapphire blue. Now you know that your energies have joined in pure and perfect intent. (Gasp, breathes heavily) Power...life.*

Tyra was shaking and shuddering as energy coursed through her body. This same energy moved through me and filled the space we were in. I began to use Light language and suggested we ask the energies to assimilate easily.

C: *I'm better now. The calf has woken up. The energy got very intense as we brought in the animated Breath of God that woke up the...(laughs). The calf is alive now and there is a celebration. I see Yeshua in the firelight. He's very jovial. We're all celebrating.*

M: What does he look like? Describe him to me.

C: *It's a little hard to see him in this light...any of us really; we're kind of shadowed. His hair is brown, kind of curly, or wavy. It's hard to see him in this light. I feel him more than see him.*

NEXT SCENE: YESHUA AND THE ROUNDTABLE COUNCIL

C: *We're at a great table. It's big. It's large with a shiny surface. There's a council there. Yeshua is speaking. He's speaking of what's ahead for his life. We're gathered as a council of supporters for him.*

M: What's he sharing?

C: *He's sharing about a time of unrest. There will be a time of sowing and reaping...the power and the potency of what's been learned. He'll go out and do the miracles, you know? He says that it's short-lived, but also eternal...something about a stone. Setting something in stone. He's talking about putting something in motion, and it's set in stone. It can't be undone or changed.*

M: What is it that's being set in stone? That's being set into motion?

C: *Energy. Christed Energy. A potential for all beings to be Christed. It's like from the stone through time things spiral outward and upward, building generation upon generation. He talks about the many changes throughout humanity. He sees what's coming and we're the council. We consider all that's being said with wisdom and sobriety.*

M: Look around the table. What do you notice about this council? Describe them to me.

C: *I don't feel like they're all human. I don't even feel all human necessarily. I feel star heritage, which feels Arcturian or something. Anyway...let's see. Who is at the table? Many masters. There's a lot of us here. It's many members of the Galactic Federation — ambassadors, many of them in human form holding the collective energy.*

Transcript: Worlds within Worlds

This next scene is a portion of another client's session describing a teaching that happened around a fire with Yeshua. There was so much in this session that may be released at a later date. For now, let us sit around the fire for a little more time with Jesus.

C: *I'm in a closed place, there's a fire in the middle. We're in a meeting. Yeshua is there. There's Anasha, Sheniha, there are these women and men, and there are also people in the background that are not in human form. They're like part of the council that is hiding. They're invisible, but I can see them. This is a big meeting, yet it is concealed in front of a fire.*

M: **Who are those first two, that you said were with you?**

C: *Anasha is like a wise woman. She's just like Magdalene, but she's not Magdalene. She's very sacred. She's very imbued with beauty. There is also Nichema who is like the brother. So, there's this, these are next to Yeshua. They're guardians, they are like guardians. They're guarding him, yeah, they keep his energy intact, so that he can do his work. So, they guard him against any disruptions in his timeline. They're also time jumpers.*

M: **So, there are other beings, you said, that have come in for this meeting as well? There are others there present?**

C: *Yeah, there are people from Orion and Sirius. They are very toned, very big in energy, and ancient. We're looking at the fire. The fire is not a fire, it's like a hologram. They're looking at all these planets and systems. They are doing a plan. From the outside, it looks like a normal fire, but when you look closely it's a window to a universe. It's like a night fire that contains many systems and stars, and it's like a window. It's like a hologram.*

M: **What are you all looking into as you look into this hologram? What are you observing?**

C: *Observing planet Earth, just observing it as it's spinning, and it's part of a bigger picture.*

M: **What is this bigger picture describing?**

C: *It's flat. There are rings. The planet, the sphere of what we know of Earth is not Earth. It is Earth, it's not as we know it. There are rings around Earth. Each ring is a world beyond Earth. The Earth is just a sphere in the middle of this, but it's part of one thing that's bigger. Earth is bigger than we think, WAY bigger. We are just inside a sphere but outside the sphere, there's more. There are rings of different nature worlds. It's really interesting.*

M: **So, these rings or are they like different versions of Earth? Or different dimensions of Earth? Are they completely different realities?**

C: *They're like Earth. They're physical. They're very real. We just don't know them. We can't see them. From the point of view of Earth, we're just floating in space but it's an illusion. Outside there are rings and each ring is a part of Earth. It's like a mountain world, a garden world, and an ice world... Yes, it's like worlds, within worlds. It's like we expand into different spheres, Earth has 13 spheres. It's like those Russian dolls, like that of Earth. Each sphere or ring will turn on for us as we progress. It's like Earth is going to be able to see the next ring and then the next ring, and then the next ring. It's like Earth is suddenly realizing its within many realities at the same time. It's that we just don't know. We don't see them but they're there. It's like we need to turn them on or like we need to be able to see them. So, there's no outer space really. It's like outer space as we see it is just a hologram. It's like a firmament. It's just a show. It's like a light show so that we can think that we are in a universe but we're not. We're contained within another sphere, within another sphere, within another sphere, 13 times.*

M: That makes sense. So, what is this group doing with this information as they watch them, what is the intention?

C: We're learning. We're learning how it works. I mean it's unveiling the truth. Like we need to know where we are. What we are really needing to do. It's like we're shut down. In the middle. It's like we're trapped in the middle like the human race is trapped in the middle.

M: So, what is Yeshua doing in the scene or these other members?

C: He's the one showing this to others in the fire. Everybody's looking at the fire. He's kind of showing them. He has the power to unveil the fire and show the others. So, they all marveled at this meeting. There are humans, and there are also nonhumans. The humans don't know that there are nonhumans. Yeah, he's just showing, he's just teaching them the reality, like the truth.

Collective Ministry Team

Jesus did not act alone in his mission. His incarnation was part of a much larger Redemption Plan involving many beings over a timespan of several generations. Many beings incarnated on the Earth to support his life's mission, and many supported from beyond the Earth. Here we stand at the culmination point of so many efforts to restore humanity and this Earth. Bless us all as we complete the restoration and manifest New Earth!

SIX

Through the Eyes of Jesus

This next client often goes into a somnambulistic trance when we work together. It was mentioned in a previous session that she would have some information about the life of Jesus to share with me. This session was remarkably unique in that the client was taken INTO the body of Jesus and Mary Magdalene at times and was able to tell me what he was thinking and feeling at different stages of his life.

I will also mention that this client knew nothing of Jesus besides from a few years of occasional church visits as a child. Everything that she shared in this transmission was brand new ideas about the life of Jesus and Mary.

C: *I see sand and water that looks like a lake, but it's not a lake, it's a sea. It's very dark, the color of the water, and the sand is also very dark; it's not like sand that you find normally on the beach. Hmm... Seems like there is a...somebody doing a ceremony there, in this water, looks like...wearing white like a priest. I think they are baptizing some kids in the sea.*

M: **What does this person in white look like?**

C: *He looks like a reminder of what happened there. He's not real. He's...he's just the...a spirit there. It's not...it's not an actual body. I just see them not touching the ground and they're just in the air and they're just white. Umm...white energy or something. And around I can see there is a priest and he's holding a baby and he told me it's a memory of what happened here. So...yeah.*

M: **What happened there?**

C: *They were doing the baptism of the kids there, in this kind of black sea that looks like a lake. It seems that this is an important place because Jesus was there. The waters are holy waters, and they used it for years for this purpose, of cleansing the impurities of the people that they would put their bodies in these waters. Like cleansing their souls, like cleansing the karma when you go into this water.*

DESCRIBES HER BODY

C: *I am...I'm flying above the lake. I don't have a body. I am...I am one with the...with Jesus's consciousness, somehow. Like I'm...I'm just spinning around observing and sometimes I see him as a vision. Comes in and out, and I'm just nowhere, but at the same time I'm all of it. I'm part of all of it, yeah.*

M: What else do you see there? What else is happening?

C: He's...he's um...I see Jesus praying there, wearing white and putting his hands on the water, like giving healing to the waters. Then a woman comes to him, she's wearing black and red. She's very beautiful and she has long dark hair. She looks like a gypsy a little bit. Dark skin, darker skin, and she's like "We have to go now, we have to go somewhere." Like, like...feels like...they're in danger. Somebody wants to...to take them somewhere, and he's like "Oh, let me finish that and we...we can go somewhere else to hide."

M: So, he's going to finish up his work with the water and then they're going to go?

C: Yeah, yeah, he's making the water holy or something.

M: How is he doing that?

C: He's just putting his hands on top of the water without even touching it. Just sending energy to the water. He is putting the christ consciousness into the water. That's why it's cleansing. He's making the... the...how to say... something that has no substance, something [that] has no... no form and puts that into the form so that it becomes that. Yeah.

M: So, he puts this new energy into the...into the water.

C: He connects the...he connects what is on the physical realm with the spiritual realm let's say. He connects the two worlds. That's what he does. He brings this energy from up there down to Earth, and he puts his energy in some sacred places so the energy can be there when he will be gone, because he knows he's going to be gone. So, this space can hold his energy still and do the work. Yeah, that's what he's doing.

M: What else do you see happening?

C: It's... I see them hugging, um...the gypsy woman and him. They're sad, but not, at the same time. They know that sadness is something very human and is...they...they feel it, but they know what is beyond all this sadness and what's the purpose and they're very serious about their purpose, and they know kind of who they are and what they came to do, and they're hiding because...actually they want to kill the woman.

M: Tell me about that.

C: So, they're hiding because she's in danger. So... she was... I don't know what she was doing but a...maybe he's not allowed to be with her for some reason.

M: I wonder why he's not allowed to be with her.

C: *Hmm...I don't know, maybe...I don't know why they're not allowed to be together, because they seem...they seem...they're...they're in love with each other and they have a good relationship, but umm...I don't know why they're not... They cannot be together somehow and there are people following, like a military to...or villagers, whatever they are, to...that's why they're hiding. He's...he's protecting her. He's taking her away from...some reason but she knows that he's going to die, and she has to stay. And that's why they're sad and they're hiding. But this sadness is not...it's...how to say it...they know...they're above their sadness. They're fine and at the same time, they're sad. They have a lot of faith. They have a lot of faith, yeah.*

NEXT SCENE: JESUS IN PRAYER

C: *This is...it comes to me in Greek, Oros Sina. This is a mountain. It's Jesus there, praying. And he seems, he lost his faith. He lost his faith; he's done with all of this. He's tired. He can't be with his love, because if he's with her they're going to kill her, so they can't be in public together very much. He lost his...his student kind of...he knows that some people will betray him and his fame about him is spreading out that he's a...it's true in what he says and he's just desperate and he's asking for help. He's asking the angels, the archangels to help him. He says, "My father denies to give me guidance." so he's calling the archangels for guidance. So, to help him, and...Gabriel comes to him. It's Gabriel above him to give him a message. He's really, really desperate; he's crying and he's losing the...it's this moment of crisis for him, where nothing works, and Gabriel tells him to trust, trust, trust. To trust who he is and what he came for on Earth and trust what he is doing and all this and...and love is something eternal; everything is love. He's falling into the human desire with the love a little bit, so it's giving him pain as well.*

M: So, he's starting to be weighed down by the human experience of being in love and...

C: *Yeah, yeah, exactly, exactly.*

M: How does he respond to Gabriel's message?

C: *He says, "That's the last time."*

M: The last time for what?

C: *I think the last time he does that or something. He's...he probably knows he's going to die soon so... He's...he's kind of done at the same time with his life, but also, he's attached to...to what others think of him and to love and to others...other emotions. He's confused now; that's why he lost the faith.*

M: How does he know that his life is coming to an end?

C: So...he heard it. He told him that.

M: Who told him?

C: I think...I think his...his...his guides...or his ancestors or...other...the ones...his family from the stars, actually, the Sirians.

M: Tell me about that.

C: He says the Sirians are involved with that.

M: How are the Sirians involved? Go see it now.

C: I think they...they say that he's one of them. He's connected with the Sirians, and he came to bring the golden light to Earth, the same you are doing here. So, he was...he kind of knew he's going to have a short life, because that was...that was the purpose, and he just did it and nothing else...sometimes when he was speaking with angels or other stuff, they say they were speaking to him as well. So, it's a...

M: So, when the angelic beings were speaking with him also these Sirian extraterrestrials were?

C: Yeah, that's what they say, that it is all connected to that, and it just comes in the form of angels sometimes but actually, also for us, as the way we can take it because we are trained to...to be...to not be afraid of them. So that's why sometimes they come in form of angels, but they are actually our brothers and sisters from Sirius or from other galaxies sometimes also, that they're here to help and you know that already — that we're helping you so...so we do the same, and we are bringing this Christ Consciousness, but the name comes from Jesus and...because he had this mission, coming to Earth, and that's how it became...but this is something very old. This is something that is part of the whole and it's always been. It's nothing new. It's just a new story to humanity but it's not new. So yeah.

M: So, tell me what's happening next with Jesus.

C: So, he's...he's going down, down from this mountain; he's walking down. He's wearing some sandals and a long white...looks like a sheet from the bed actually, like a weird white thing with some gold strap here. Like ancient Greek a little bit also, looks like. He's covered his head; his head is covered with this white, like this, like the women do, the Eastern women and he seems like he got some power from this mountain. He seems like...determined to just go and do it, so he's going to find his students and prepare a special ceremony and talk to them about something, so he's going to do this now...ahhh...he's going to tell the students that he's going to die.

M: Tell me about it. What do you see happening there?

C: But he's going to come back afterward, so he's...he has to tell the students what he received at the mountain, the message kind of. Yeah, he will die, and they'll have to continue the work after he leaves. So, what...that's what he is going to do and the girl, the girlfriend or whatever...she is there as well, in the dinner, they're all there, all there, the students and her and...

M: Describe the room to me. What else is going on?

C: Maybe she's...maybe she's also a student of his, maybe she's also a student somehow, um...

M: What's happening in that room? Describe it to me. Is there a dinner?

C: It's...it seems like a very basic place, very poor. Seems like everybody is spread out; they're not all sitting at a table. They're spread out in this room, and they have a little table between two or three people and everybody seems worried. Mary Magdalene [first time she is called by her name] is touching the feet of Jesus and feeling very sad and then I see somebody eating an apple; there's...there are some animals also at the back there. Looks like a farmhouse or something. Looks very much...very basic...I don't know if it's wood, but it looks like destroyed wooden walls, and it's not really food; it's not like the dinners we have. They just have bread and olives I see. It's just very basic, and wine, red wine. And some fruit, they have fruits.

M: So, he's sharing the news with them?

C: Yes, so they're all...all spread out in the room, and they have a little food, and he's like "Come together, sit down." They are all sitting down, like in a circle, not on a table, on the floor, and he's like "You have to know, you have to know who you are, you have to know what you came here to do and nobody... nobody's superior to you. We're all one, and we are doing the same, and now I have to leave, and one of you will betray me for...for divine order, because it has to happen this way." without putting any shame or guilt to this person that will do it, because he has to do it for some higher purpose. And they're like, um...they're just freaking out with this information, and they're crying and Mary Magda...Mary Magdalene I said?

This woman... Maybe they became really furious, and she's...she's very cool about it. She's not reactive. She's sitting there, like she knows already these things; she's not reactive, and she's actually trying to understand who is going to do it, who is going to do the betrayal and she's very strong in her intuition, and she's looking to understand and it's...it's a man that looks very...a little bit ugly actually. Short, very...looks like he works in nature; he has a very strong body and also destroyed a little bit, from the sun, from scratches. He has curly black hair; his eyes are black, and he's...his face is kind of ugly... like... she recognized him, that it's him, he...he's going to do it. And he's angry, but he seems...you know they just look at their eyes kind of and he got it that she knows that it's going to be him and he's just behaving like weird...kind of, but the other ones, they don't understand that it's him, just like...being next to Jesus and trying to touch him and say "No, this is...maybe you got it wrong; this is not happening." So that's what's happening and...and they're just, um...trying to find a solution and he is saying that "This is nothing to find a solution for. This is the way it has to be; it's divine order; it's the law of the universe; it's the law of God."

M: How is this the law of God and law of the universe? Does he explain that?

C: *Yeah, it's more like, it's all one and it has to...when something is not balanced some people have to come and bring the balance. The same with you guys, so it's like it's not balanced and it's a lot of war, a lot of killing, a lot of bad things happening back then, so he had to come to show love, that nobody else would talk about that before. So when the unbalance comes, somebody has to do...somebody or something has to come and do the work with the balance and he's...he's very much connected with...with the Sirius planet and it's very high intelligence beings that come and take on human forms through reincarnations and sometimes it's not just reincarnations, sometimes they just go in and out of human bodies just to be in certain missions [walk-ins], so they also do that.*

M: So sometimes they just walk in?

C: *Yeah, yeah, they do. They do. They can't really interfere. They can't really do much, but if you are sensitive you can feel them sometimes around and...it's hard for them also to show the way they look, because they don't want to scare you but when you see blue auras around they probably are them, even if you think that they're angels, it's just Sirians most of the times, yeah, not all of them...blue aura, yeah.*

NEXT SCENE: ANGRY JESUS

C: I see...Jesus is very angry and he's going inside a temple and destroying the temple. He's doing that. He's very angry. It's a lot of cages with birds and stuff, and...ahh...they're doing, sacrificing animals there in this temple...probably... And he's like "What are you doing, why are you doing these things?" and he doesn't understand why they're doing these things and like they're killing these animals; they have these temples but they're still idiots, kind of, you know? So, he's...he's...he got super angry, very angry, and he's saying, "In the name of God I'm taking this down." and he's kicking, screaming, trying to...to destroy the temple and he's kind of done with the humans (laughs), seems like he's really like "These guys are really...they don't get it." Yeah, yeah, yeah.

M: And how does everyone respond as he has his temper tantrum?

C: Yeah, they're...they are looking like, freaked out, like what is he doing, you know? And some of them, they're saying, "He must be the Messiah, because he behaves this way, nobody ever did this way." Some of them really follow him afterward when he leaves and [they] say, "Tell us, what should we pray to, what should we do, because these gods didn't help; help us, look what is happening here." And he says "Ok, follow me and I'll show you." And some others, they stayed at the back and they're just like freaked out by what he did to the temple, you know? And they're going to call the militaries, militaries or whatever they are, ones from the village to search for him and see what's going on, why he...how he can do that to them.

NEXT SCENE: A WALK-IN EXPERIENCE

C: He's doing energy healing work. It's a woman that is not feeling well and they're desperate. They call him to help her and he's doing energy healing; he's not touching the body, he's just sending energy with his hands. Seems she's getting awake, she's alive now. She was dead...so she was dead or something or she was...she seems...she seems pretty good, like he just gave her the Light again, the light of life.

M: How does that work?

C: Yeah, this is weird what he does. He's reactivating the light inside the heart. So everybody has a light in the heart or this is closed, is blocked, and his role was to really light that flame from in the heart and so white light...white-golden light in the heart, and some people had to die because they were very closed in the heart and they couldn't stay and they were also um...creating more trouble for the other ones to find the light. So, it was like a big pandemic back then and a lot of people died from...from disease, because of that, because it had to clear up all the souls.

M: So, people were dying because their heart was closed?

C: I mean...kind of what's happening now, similar thing with the virus. Like some people had to...some souls have to leave because their heart is very closed and they're not helping the others to rise, also they're really putting the energy down, so they just have to leave. That's what happened back then as well, the same thing.

M: So, it's similar to what's happening now?

C: Yeah, it's very similar; it's very similar.

M: So, tell me what you're seeing...yeah, what you're seeing there?

C: And the Sirians are helping now as well, very much. That's why they're bringing so many um...let's say souls or intelligence from there.

M: So, Jesus was bringing this woman back to life? What do you see happening now?

C: Yeah, yeah. He's um...he's doing what I'm doing (moving hands in the air in mudras), but I don't know what I'm doing but he's doing this (laughs). He's doing this... and he's bringing back the Light. He's activating the Light in the heart. It's a...and this woman is like (coughs)...she's coughing and she's coming back to life, and her face looks young and beautiful and...she was very old before and now she's... she's still old, but she seems like the Light made her so beautiful, so different like a new soul came inside of her or something like that. So, what he says to me is that what he did, he let the old soul go to reincarnate somewhere else and he brought a new soul straight into the body. So, this woman will continue for a purpose to share the story but is another soul that came in. The other one actually died and a new one came, and this is a very common thing that you guys experienced already; it's happened also to you — where a different part of your consciousness came in.

M: What do you mean that we understand because it happened to us?

C: Like in terms of the person you were like ten years ago and the person you are now. It's a completely different consciousness and you can see that. That's exactly the same. You couldn't operate now with your old consciousness, so it had to recede and it had to die, and it had to die through a very strong depression, or that's how it dies usually or something that really hurts you or in...in the life, some events that put you really down and it allows this old thing to die and a...it's a different process for you guys because you have a different path than others but briefly it was like that. That's what Jesus was doing, and he was...he was working on the chakras that are the energy centers of the human body; he will open them one by one and connect them to the heart and open the heart. And this woman can spread this Light now, she has it already.

M: That's wonderful.

C: That's the...that's the plan. The mission.

M: Very good.

C: He is putting three crosses on the heart, to seal it.

M: And what is this symbolism of the three crosses? How does that work?

C: This is the beginning of everything. This is like um...how all this got manifested. 'Because everything started from being nothing, it manifested like a little dot in the center and the first manifestation was like the cross, like the feminine and masculine energies then created the rest. This is the beginning of everything. This is a symbol also you can use for sealing your energy when you need to make a cross on your body. That will seal your energy field and keep it inside, keep it protected.

NEXT SCENE: SHIFTING INTO MARY

C: I feel and...I'm not Jesus anymore. I am...I feel I'm shifting between being him and the woman, because I'm...I'm feeling now anxious and I'm going to die then I'm going back into...I'm going in and out in different bodies I feel. So, I'm once the woman and once him and um...now I'm feeling very anxious because I feel I'm in the body of Jesus and he is walking barefoot and holding his cross going to the mountain to die, and then the woman... The woman behind is following the crowd, but he's...she's keeping a distance, so they don't recognize her somehow. Yeah.

M: How does it feel to be Jesus as he's on this walk? What does his inner guide feel like?

C: He's a...feeling a ha...a hand...on his head, giving him trust and support and saying this is an illusion and don't worry about the death because there's no death and you know about it in the first place, and he's telling him that he's one with Maria; he's never going to lose her because they're one and even when he dies he can be with her because he will see it from a higher perspective and he will understand that. Now he is in his human desires. He can't really have clarity because of that, but this is going to end soon, and he has to see it as a liberation, not as something that is a punishment to him because he's only done good, so he doesn't have to feel guilty. He has to release this...the guilt and see it as a liberation process and really just have fun with...because he knows the truth and he's...he's crying.

M: And how is this for Mary? What is she going through as she follows?

C: She...she's very intuitive as I said, and she knows...she kind of knows already everything. She...she knows...she has this deeper knowing; she understands why this is happening and it's something beyond her desire to be with him, and she's...she has a lot of compassion and he's used her kind of strength in the same time like she's experiencing the deep sadness indeed, but some part of it knows that this is not real anyway; it's an illusion. She's fighting between two worlds.

M: And how does it feel in the crowd as he moves through? What does it feel like as he moves through this place?

C: The crowds are horrible. They're very angry. They're throwing things at him and screaming at him. They...it seems like they hate him.

M: Why do they hate him?

C: Because, um...they don't understand him. First, they think he's crazy, but then they think he's arrogant crazy, and then they think he's spiritually arrogant crazy. So, at these times this was not permitted, and he was speaking badly about their religion and beliefs and that was not permitted to happen back then, so...people...the human life didn't have so much...it was not precious so much these years. So, it was...it's not like now, they can kill like...for nothing. So, when somebody was different, they would kill him. Yeah, something like that.

NEXT SCENE: GOING TO THE CRYPT

C: I hear Mary Magdalene saying, "Let's go to the crypt." She's going... He's...he's already out of the body and she wants to go to the place his body is or something, because she wants to see what happened. She's sure that something is going to happen there. She's very happy actually. She's super happy and she says, "He told me, he's going to be there, let's go." and she's talking with another woman, older than her. She seems also very spiritual, like really into it, and they're going there; they're wearing black and it's a...illumination of...it's the body of Jesus is...it's..how to say...energy body, it is white energy, you can still see that it's him and he's changing faces to me now, he's like... I can see different...like Osiris; I can see Shiva; I can see different ones right...changing constantly like shuuu! They're very happy, they're just blind from the Light and he's saying, "There is no death. It's an illusion; you are the first to witness it and you are women, that's why you are the first to witness it."

M: Why are the women the first?

C: Because the women are more receptive, they're more connected, more understanding to spirituality than men, especially at these periods and because one was his love and the other was...I don't know, looks like a mother or something, or something from the family, so it was the dearest women of his life.

M: What happened to the physical body in the process once he was put into the crypt?

C: It's...I hear in Greek...the answer. It's called...it's...I don't know what to...how to translate it. Aya...ayase? It's like when somebody becomes a saint and the body becomes holy and kind of dissolves, because it has to show that is...when the body is holy it just dissolves somehow, that's what I hear. It just disappears somehow, dissolves, I see, disappears...and then...I don't know why it does that, that is what I hear, and he's... He's a...he's um...he's, he's showed himself on his kind of energy body, Lightbody, and he's very big as well, very big; he's very big, like...they're...they're blind from that...from the Light; it's big. It's like apocalyptic... It's like...whoa!

M: What was happening while his physical body was going through its dissolving process? What was his Lightbody doing?

C: He's...I see he is laying on the back; the physical body just starts (makes crumbling sounds) disappearing like this, eating...eating itself, and then the white soul body, it's a white body, just comes out of the tomb and rises up, and it's just in the air now. And he says, "I can be anywhere now." He doesn't have to walk; he can just be anywhere now. Like...seems like he's...tele...telekinesis. He's going very fast to different places, yeah.

M: So, he's able to travel anywhere very quickly?

C: Yeah, yeah, yeah, yeah.

M: So, when he appears to the women what happens next?

C: So, they...they're very happy. It confirms their faith and everything they were receiving. All the information they were also receiving from the angels, confirms what happened, and um...they're just very happy and very like...wow, it's true what he was saying. Like...they start believing... I mean, they believed even but now it's like whoa... "We have to give this... they ha... We have to tell the other students." And they had to tell the other students also and this has to be in books, in...it has to spread, this information. Slowly, because they will kill them as well, they have to be careful in the beginning, especially Mary has to be very careful.

M: So, what do they do?

C: Um... She decides to spend some time in isolation, so she will just process whatever happened and try to get guidance and hide to protect herself. Seems she's having a kid or something.

M: So, she's pregnant?

C: Hmm...seems like. She's...she's going into a cave to give birth to this baby that nobody has to know.

M: So, she's going to give birth to this child?

C: So, she's in the cave. She's pregnant. She's very happy. She's trusting as never before. She knows that she has to protect this kid, and she knows that she's going to die very soon as well. She knows she's not going to live very long for some reason. They know everything (laughs), and then what I see is they're sitting there and seems like some students are taking care of her. Like, she's in an isolated place, but they're going to bring her food. She's there with some animals. She's meditating all days; she's a refugee, like...protected there. And the baby is...needs to like...nobody needs to know about it and...

M: And why should nobody know about the baby?

C: Because they were not supposed to be together. Because he was a teacher, she was like...a woman from a...bad neighborhood or something I hear. Like not a very great background. Like she was from a place where very poor people live, they had no good behavior towards each other, a lot of violence...and they mistreated women there very much, so...

M: Has she given birth to the child yet?

C: She's um...she's having the pain now. And Jesus is there; he's there...like well...white (in his Lightbody form) He's supporting the process and talking to her. She's just freaking out (laughs) that she sees that.

M: How is he supporting the process?

C: He's...he's there for her, standing in front of her and he's...seems like he's taking out the baby and holding it with his hands somehow, and he also says nobody has to know about that. Because if they knew, they would kill the baby, that's the thing. They would kill the baby if they knew about the baby.

M: So, tell me about this baby. What do you notice about it?

C: It's like um...it's blond, with curly hair and blue eyes. It doesn't look like her at all. She's more dark-skinned and brown, you know. They spend a lot of time there in isolation with animals and support of students bringing food and support there. It seems that she's sick now. The baby is like five or something.

M: And what is the sex of this baby?

C: He's a boy. Yeah, I see a boy, yeah. She knows she's going to die and what it's going to do...she's worried about the baby. She's doing some channeling and asking what to do. One of the students, he's going to have to take care of the baby. I hear Yacov, in Greek, I don't know what it is. So probably him, he's going to take care of the baby. She has to leave the body for some reason and the baby is going to learn with the student of him and be now undercover and continue the work for him. That's what he says.

Christ-Magdalene Bloodline

The bloodline of Yeshua and Mary had to be protected to secure the ascension of humanity. I imagine that part of the reason why information regarding the precise number of children is blurry has to do with the information being enshrouded to protect the lineage.

It is similar to how some psychic information is being blocked or limited when looking at the future ascension timelines. Many beings would do harmful actions if they had the exact information, so I believe the information is being "fragmented" to protect the work that has been done thus far with the genetic enhancements. More will come out over these next years!

SEVEN

Esther the Essene

I had the pleasure of working with Neomi several times over a few years both in-person and remotely via video conferencing software. When I work with clients repeatedly, I use a keyword to induce them quickly into a trance state. As I say the agreed-upon phrase, the client immediately begins to drop into a hypnosis trance. I can tell because the face and body posture soften, their eyes begin to flutter, and the energy of the room begins to shift. At this point, I can either suggest that we move to a specific time and place, or I can ask that we be taken to the most appropriate time for us to learn. Typically, I like to use the second option so that the higher realms can show me what is most important to be shown. After researching what "spontaneously" shows up, I guide the client to specific times that I want to research. Most of the times that I did this with Neomi, she most often went back to the same lifetime as Esther.

Esther lived in a small, private community that seemed to be a spiritual community. Her mother and teachers taught her to work with herbs for healing. As she grew up, she was taught more advanced skills of meditation and telekinesis, moving objects with her mind. There was a powerful storyline including a deep bond with her sister and best friend, Rae. As a young girl, Esther was abused and raped and ended up producing a child, a young boy named Josiah who she gave to another healer in the area who would raise the boy and train him in advanced psychic and esoteric arts. She described the woman as a powerful medicine woman who wore raven feathers in her hair. In the middle of the second session, she gave me the name of her community and the story of her relationship with Jesus began to be told.

What you will read here is a reduced summary of all of the sessions I did with Esther. Esther deserves her own book and maybe someday I will get to it. For now, I share with you some of the lost stories of Jesus through the eyes of his dear friend and student, Esther.

Esther shared that the human collective at the time was extremely polarized and fear-based. The Romans and the rabbis spread messages of fear throughout the region. Jesus had been traveling through the region sharing teachings of love, faith, and community, and people were beginning to come together as Jesus seeded these new ideas into the collective consciousness.

The first scene was when she was a young girl, maybe four or five years old, and Jesus has come to visit her community, which she calls Qumran. Jesus meets with each family and marks certain members of each family, children included, with a cross on their forehead by gesturing with his hands. He explains to young Esther as he marks her that she will be working with him in the future to do healing work.

When I move her forward to the next scene, she is a bit older and is working for a "king" in the kitchen of what she calls a palace close to the temple. She secretly works with different people by doing hands-on healing work and sharing spiritual guidance. While working in the kitchen, there is a lot of excitement about an important visitor who is coming to meet with one of the rabbis for a Passover dinner. The rabbi shares that "The Nazarene is coming!" Esther is confused because she had never heard of a man with this title and the rabbi was acting like a king is coming over.

When Jesus arrives, she comments on how bright his energy is. Jesus recognizes her energy signature that she holds and remembers her from Qumran. He requests that she gather a few women together to meet privately later that evening in the kitchen.

NEXT SCENE: MEETING WITH THE WOMEN

C: *We were able to gather nine women, so there are eleven of us together, and we have drinks for all of them, water, and some bread. He comes in, and he's just so glad to see us all. He has us stand together in a giant circle and hold hands. The kitchen is very...it's generously large here, so we are able to do that. He has us bow our heads and breathe in and center ourselves and just feel how united we are together, and to feel our hearts combine together as one.*

So, we breathe into this meditation, and as we do you can just feel...just a warm, warm energy ripple through everyone — through our hands and through our hearts, and it just feels like we're on a different plane. It's just so amazing. So, he has us breathe into this for quite a while, and we just all sit down together in a large circle, and he asks us if anyone has any questions...if anything has come up that they have any specific questions on.

One woman raises her hand and says that it's so hard to believe in anything when the soldiers come around so often and then the rabbis ask for things. So, she feels she has so little, that it is so difficult to keep going some days knowing that she's just working so hard, long hours, just to have everything taken.

He says, "Well, did you have adequate food today and shelter?" And she says, "Yes." He says, "How are your neighbors? Did you speak with them today?" She says, "Yes." And he says, "Do you have a loving family around you?" And she says, "Yes. I do." And he says, "You have all of these things. You have love. You are so rich." He said there are others who don't even have a fraction of that and to possibly consider every morning upon waking, just pause...pause and maybe kneel down and go inward. Think of the things that are surrounding her and be grateful for just a little while before starting her day. Just that small amount of gratefulness and love and appreciation for everything will spread throughout the day.

If you don't find...if you just find it difficult to keep going...just turn to your neighbor or to your family and just speak to them...and ask them for some uplifting words. So many people keep the fear inside and if you would just speak up and ask. Just tell your neighbor how you feel; they'll be more than happy to give an uplifting word, or maybe invite you over for a moment and just listen. If we can all stay together as one and unite in love, every day will be easier to go on. Have faith. When you don't have faith, just maybe kneel down and go inward. Just go inward and feel that light that's within you.

You, as women, have the most amount of intuition and you can feel the subtle differences in energies and people's feelings. So, when you go out, if you see in someone's eyes that their light is slightly dim, then approach them and ask them if they can use a hug or would they like to talk. Just reach out to them. I think that will help everyone to stay together.

If you hear any new information, speak with each other and spread that energy information, and just sit with each other. Don't isolate yourself. If the soldiers come by, that is difficult, but just know...don't lament in it. Just know that tomorrow is another day, and you are loved, and you have light inside you, and you can spread that light. In each day you can choose to do so, or you can choose to live in fear. When you choose to spread that light, that light will grow, and it will touch one person to the next person to the next and create this grand light, this loving light, and the kindness will spread. And eventually, the soldiers' grip will weaken on everyone. They won't be able to keep up a stronghold for very long. The kingdom will crumble. So, keep faith within each other so you can rise up and live in peace and ease one day. Know that it is coming.

He's saying that he must leave. If we have any questions...but everyone seems satisfied with the lessons he has talked to them about. He did go on to say that everyone is capable of healing with their hands — that their hands are another chakra, and so he encouraged us women to get together regularly and speak to each other and possibly, just work with our hands. I know how to do the healing, so I think I'll try to lead up the women's group and show them the general steps of how to work with healing energy.

I'm very intimidated by this because we're supposed to be...we have to be discreet. We have to be very discreet. There are nine other women here besides my sister and me, but I believe if we meet a few times, we can gain trust within the group, and I can show them the healing so that they can go out and spread the healing, even if they start with their families and move outward. But if they can heal and work with the children especially, so that the children have this knowledge and then they can go out and just change how things are when they're older. That maybe they can go against the grain and understand that there doesn't need to be separation, even though there will be for a long, long, long, long time, but just putting the idea in their heads of the equality and the healing — that they're able to heal themselves and have faith. So, the women are disbursing and they're leaving.

NEXT SCENE: WALKING THROUGH JERUSALEM

C: We're in Jerusalem. On my way home though, I see a man speaking with some of the council for the temple...and then I realize, it's Jesus. He notices me...you know...I have to walk past them. So, I'm walking up and he looks at me and says, "I'll talk to you later on this afternoon." But he doesn't say it out loud. It's telepathic. So, I acknowledge that, and I walk past, and I go to my living quarters...

So later on in the evening Rae and I go into the temple to eat. So, she comes back, and we go in to do that and we're...We got there late so we missed the supper with everyone, so we just grab some of the leftover food and we're just eating. And he [Jesus] enters in the kitchen and he just talks to us briefly. He acknowledges us because he knew us from when we lived with our parents in Qumran. So, we're just chatting with him nonchalantly. So, he's going to be *staying at the temple for three days, and he just asked if we'd like to sit in on the women's meeting. So, we'd love to do that, so we'll meet up tomorrow. So, we'll see him then.*

NEXT SCENE: A CLASS ON SELF HEALING FROM JESUS

C: *Well, there's a handful of women and we're in someone's home. He's saying thank you so much for coming because I know that...this sort of set-up for women in the city is frowned upon. He thanks us for coming and for being discreet. He's just so happy to see us. So, he just wants to talk to us about some updated teachings that he has. He said he was traveling in the far, far East. He said he wanted to talk to us about energy work and channeling the divine into yourself to heal yourself. So, he wanted to show us some basic things and go over them to help us with stuff to use.*

M: What did he share with you?

C: *He started talking about going into meditation. He has his hands at heart center and he's just looking down. His gaze is towards his fingertips and he's just breathing in, starting to relax. He's sitting upright. Then he starts going into a chant. He's saying, "Om Shanti." So, he's chanting that a few times, and then he picks his head up and he puts his hands down on his knees and he just starts breathing. And he explains to us to breathe in and breathe in all the air around you and pull your energy inward. So, he's showing us how to breathe in, inhaling in, and pulling your energy inward, and exhaling that just around you so that your energy is concentrated inward towards you.*

Then he's saying, if we could lie back, if there's enough room, and start by placing your hands on your heart. Then he's showing us to breathe in there and feel any changes and to fully, fully relax and to release any fears that we may have and just understand that everything is God's will and divine plan and it's set up. So, we mustn't worry about things that don't make sense to worry about because it's out of our control.

(This next part seems more comfortable sitting upright.) Then he's having us put our hands upon our shoulders and he's saying to breathe in here and to open your elbows outward...so don't crunch over, so be open to the energy and breathing in here. He's inviting us to feel the energy flowing down our hands, down our fingertips, and back into us. And he's explaining its divine energy.

Then he's putting his hands on the back of his neck, down by your spine and he's breathing in there. And then he has his hands go up behind his head. So, putting his thumbs in the little notch in the base of the skull and all of his fingers...so all four fingers pointing upward towards the crown. So, he's like pressing into the zeal and then he's directing the energy upwards towards the crown and having it stay there.

And then putting the hands on the head...so your fingertips are pointing up towards the back of your head and your thumbs are outward...and breathing in there. Then over your face, touching right above your eyebrows and cupping your hands over your eyes. Then at the jaw...and then down at your solar plexus, sacral chakra, and root chakra and then out to your hips. And then bending one leg at a time and holding each foot...and staying a really long time at your feet.

And then bringing your knees to your chest and running your hands from your feet all the way up to your knees and then extending your legs and running your hands up your whole entire body, all the way up, past your crown and extending your hands and breathing in the divine energy all through you. So, he's showing us how to do that.

And then afterwards, when we're feeling energetic...if people are ill or things of that nature, working with them. So that's what he went over and then he said he'd follow up and teach us more the next time he comes...because he's supposed to be going and learning more information soon. So, he'll have more to share with us...and keep us up to date.

Then some people are asking about his journey, if he will, in fact, be coming through because it seems like there is pressure on him by the soldiers and government and people in charge. But he said he'll be able to still come through, nonchalantly...and keep teaching us so we can work behind the scenes to heal people.

M: Does he share where he will be traveling to?

C: *He said it's far, far off into the East. So, he said it would be months before he was back, but he was already there for a few months, so he learned the beginnings of this energy work. So, he wanted to share it with everybody and then he'll go for further training soon when he was ready. So, this is wonderful, because you can definitely feel the energy pulsing through you and such a connection, so this will be wonderful to share with people and I think they'll be very receptive to it.*

M: Wonderful. You said he was working with other people and

helping them with their illnesses. How's he doing that? Tell me what happened.

C: *He's going by each person and speaking with them, and it's typically...if someone has an illness, it's usually because they have an imbalance that's manifested into their body. So, he'll usually speak to them and find out what spiritual dis-ease they have and speak with each person to reassure them of Spirit and then by holding their hands and using this energy that he is channeling, he's able to work to heal the person. But it's usually never of the body, it's of the spirit.*

NEXT SCENE: LEARNING WITH JESUS

C: *He [Jesus] comes to my women's meetings when he comes into town. He always speaks at them. He has just come back from the Far East, and this has been his fourth time there. So, he has shown us different mudras with your hands and just a few basics that he has learned the last time. He was telling us some mantras, but he was really explaining last time about meditation and how that was the most important way to connect with Source and the universal energy and the Light. The pure, pure loving Light.*

So, everyone is sitting on blankets and he's getting comfortable on a blanket in front of the room and I'm sitting beside him. He asks if anyone has had any experiences with their meditations where they have had visions other than their surroundings.

A woman raises her hand and says that yes, she's experienced seeing different beings and was confused on what that was because it wasn't anything that she's seen and it was slightly alarming, but they meant no harm. He said as you get into your meditations you may start to travel. He explained to us that though we were "fresher" so-to-speak to the Earth that we had had other lifetimes and so many times you'll travel to those lifetimes. He made us aware that you could ask questions. You could explore in the lifetime when you're in your meditation, and if anything alarming comes up, then just slowly come out or just observe it with love.

So, he was explaining this to us, and he was saying that we had...with using our energy work so much...and doing the work, meditating, and having a regular discipline that we would see more and more but then also, on occasion, see less in others. Not seeing them as lesser but seeing less in their eyes. That as we brightened and became more awake, we would notice when someone was not awake yet and there would be a dullness within them. What was most important was that it was our job to be friends with those people and be kind and just glowing and radiating this oozing, positive light so that they would be intrigued by it. Then, possibly, down the road being able to offer them a healing or praying with them...offering to pray with them to help bring this awareness and awakening to them.

So now that we were at that point where we were experiencing visions, it was now time to share it with others in a friendly manner that they would understand, to be nonchalant. That was most important. That's what he was learning in the Far East is to interact with others, naturally, but yet weaving in the Light so that it was slowly resonating with them and bringing them to a conscious awareness. He invited us to go out and subtly work with others and interact with them. He said it will be difficult and just be as nonchalant as possible, slowly weaving it in.

So, a lot of us, you know, the people there being women, we're hustling through our work throughout the day and feeding people and this and that. So, he said it will take the utmost patience, so we need to step back and just be patient and just keep weaving it in and keep weaving it in and just like a weaver weaves, we will have beautiful, beautiful cloth full of light and just the most radiant, beautiful light by the end of our lifetimes and that's why we're here. That's the point, our purpose here this lifetime. It sounded simple enough but very difficult to undertake. Especially in the area where we were living in because we just had to be nonchalant about our work as it is.

NEXT SCENE: MEETING WITH JESUS AND MARY

C: All the women, and it's a huge group — much bigger than when we first started. There are maybe forty women just crammed into our kitchen area and we are waiting for Jesus to come and talk to us and let us know the new information he received from the East. And we're talking amongst ourselves. Our focus, mainly, is the exploration of the energy work. There is a handful of women, the ones I usually go talk to, that are masters in different aspects. And we're trying to teach everybody how to get back to those original abilities. So, I am excited to see what Jesus will say about any new modalities we are able to incorporate or add, maybe that I could learn.

Finally, he's arrived. We allow him to come in and have some water and rest a moment from his travels. I go over to him and embrace and express...wait a minute...entering in with him is Mary! She has never come to one of our meetings before!

M: Describe her to me. What does she look like?

C: She has this radiant energy. She has this kind of olive-ish skin, long, dark hair and is slender. You can tell she radiates this indescribable mystic energy. Just really...she's very indescribable. She comes in and smiles, and she's wearing a cloak. She slides down the hood and all the ladies are in awe because we didn't know she was going to come as well.

She has large gold hoop earrings. There's an Egyptian look to her as she has on her face lining around her eyes and some green mineral on her eyelids, but not heavily, just really lightly. She just looks really regal and beautiful, and yet, very humble and just like one of us.

So, Jesus starts laughing because I am so surprised she is there. And he's like, yes, he just wanted to wait a moment until she came in. He knew I would be excited to meet her. So, I go over and embrace her, and you can just feel this radiant energy pulse through you when you touch her.

And she just wanted to come tonight to talk. The palace has a huge staff, so she wanted to slide in as one of the staff so that she could work with us for the next three or four days so that we could learn the energy work that she and Jesus use to assist people in healing, but also to shift their perspective so that they understand that they're not needing to be held down by the rules of the palace and the city. That they can transcend the mundane and they can rise above them, and it doesn't need to be in a violent or way of an upheaval, just in their regular, everyday lives. We are just elated.

Jesus starts to talk about how he went east and worked with the monks but there were also people visiting from the Far East visiting the monks that he worked with as well. So, it was kind of a culmination of Chinese and new energy. A lot of the women know a little bit about energy work, so he just goes over breathing and a meditation practice to connect to the energy as usual and things that we already know to do with the hands and that.

He said that he had a new energetic overlay that allowed him to increase his frequency and vibration, so he wanted to pass that to each of us so that our energy would be enhanced, and he was going to show us how to do that energetic overlay. He uses me as his model for this.

He puts one hand on my chin and one hand on my crown, well a little bit more towards the back than that, and he starts there and then he covers both ears. Then he has one hand on the back of my head, on my occipital ridge, and then one on my third eye.

And then he places his left hand over my heart in front. The feminine he said. And then the backside of you, being the will, his right hand — the male aspect. And so, he places his left hand on my heart and his right hand on the back of my heart chakra, on my back.

And here in the work, he does the overlay. He is just breathing, and you can feel the energy going through him and right into my body. And so, I feel this most like, what nowadays it would look like, a digital overlay of a person laying on this radiant gold, yet there's an intertwining of a blue, like a light teal — a beautiful, radiant blue, with it as well.

So, I feel such a huge difference after this. And just with those hand motions, the opening up of the pineal gland to help bring this energy into the heart is the purpose of touching the head so I can work with all of the glands to help inform the aura and all of the energetic layers...about guiding them, about letting the energy guide the person.

This energy is just radiating through me so much I can barely speak to the group or anyone. It's as if my skin is shaking...vibrating, and I can feel my bones become warm. I can feel it in my heart, just this radiant opening. I can physically feel it, and I can feel the energy rise up my spine, all the way to the crown of my head. And it fuses each chakra as it goes up with the radiant new energy. It's really almost overwhelming, and yet it feels so good.

He's laughing and putting his hand on my shoulder and asking if I am okay. I tell him I just need a minute. The ladies give me some water. He said it's a very moving practice. After engaging with someone you should probably let them rest for a while, to assist with the energy.

For the sake of the meeting, I attempt to re-ground myself. He tells us that Mary is going to stay with us for a few days so that she can work with people individually. And as we learn how to do that, spread it amongst our group and do it to each other and infuse each person with this...this new overlay of energy, to raise the vibration in the city because there are so many ladies here, and then we're encouraged to work with others.

There are many people that the ladies work with, but we can't have everyone come to the meeting as we don't have enough space. But my skin is still buzzing. My bones feel so warm, they are almost hot. I feel like I am levitating.

In this next scene, Esther is reunited with her son Josiah whom Esther had previously sent to be raised by another woman who wore black raven feathers in her hair who was to teach Josiah advanced healing and psychic skills.

NEXT SCENE: TRAVELING WITH JESUS AND MARY

C: I have gone back from the meeting to the Essenes' community with Jesus and Mary. We worked with everybody and they're going to do these overlays. He brought me back because he and Mary wanted to talk to me about something. They wanted to ask if I would travel with them south, towards Egypt.

I ask what the purpose of this trip was, and he said he wanted to work with the energy of the pyramids and gain insight from a contact that he had there. He thought the ladies had their meetings and that handled, but it was time for me to do some other things now and to travel around to teach.

I tell him I will return back the next day with my answer. He will be there for a few more days so there is no rush. I enjoy looking into the other rooms of the community and see the younger people get training on things that I know.

And then I ask Josiah...he coordinates, or matches, the children with the masters. There are so many masters there that know different things; they are experts in different modalities. And so, Josiah can intuitively tell what strength each child has, or young person, and then he matches them with the master.

And Josiah is much older now...and so I wonder what happened to him after he left the woman with the raven feathers. So, he is managing that. So, I talk with him at length 'cause that's my son and I ask him how he is doing and it's wonderful to see him.

And he invites me, instead of going back, if I would just write a letter to my sister to make arrangements so I can stay in his quarters so we can refresh our connection. So, I tell him yes, that would be wonderful, so I compose a letter to my sister, and they send a courier. The courier has to travel at night because the Roman soldiers are still out there. They are hanging out amongst the rocks now. They are not stirring up or doing anything.

So, I ask him what new things the masters are teaching since I have last been there. It's been quite a while. And he was delighted to show me. And we go into different rooms, and in the first room, he told me well before we were at the doorway, on approaching, to be extremely quiet. One master was working with this young child, and he was levitating an orb above the table. Scrying into it.

So, the master was showing him what his lesson was for today — how to move the orb — to move it to the left, to the right, to try to control it with his mind. So, I watched that for quite a while; it was wonderful.

And then the next room, he said that this is new and slightly controversial within the community. The master was working with the child to move air. Well, they're not in a room, they are in a courtyard. And in the courtyard, this master was working with this child to control the weather, so if they needed a cloud to come by for shade, or something of that nature, is what they were working on in the sky.

And it wasn't seen upon as evil, it was just very...obviously because they were teaching it, there were just some questions attached to that. But there was only one child that was able to work with it, so it would never be in a negative way obviously. But in conversation people debate and ask questions about it.

So, it's getting to be supper time and he says he'll show me more in the morning, and we just go to eat with everyone, and we just catch up, and I stay. And in the morning my sister was waiting for the courier, and she sent a letter straight back encouraging me to travel and she would take care of everything and why would I even worry about it, but I am so close to her it is almost like we are one sometimes and it is hard to separate.

So, after we break our fast in the morning, I am drinking water and some small amount of cheese and vegetables; I talk with Mary and Jesus and tell them I will be embarking with them on their trip. And so, I enjoy some time to relax with Josiah before I need to get ready to go.

They have extra clothing and all sorts of things and so I don't need to go back to the palace to get my things. And since I've come along in this life, I used to carry talismans with me, and I just see no need for that anymore. I just like to do the work directly.

I accept the clothing they have in the community and enjoy an evening with Josiah, and we are to head out in the morning. And there is some talk about whether the soldiers are going to disrupt anything, and so we decided last minute to go ahead and leave at night. And it will be much cooler then anyway. I hug my son and we head out onto this journey.

The journey is so long. I know we will get there, but it just seems that it's taking so long. But what breaks up the monotony is that we are able to stop and visit different people in different cities, so that's been wonderful. I spend more time talking with Mary at length. We know all the same energy work and healing techniques already, but she radiates this different, purer vibration and it's so wonderful to be in her presence.

She has such a pleasant disposition. Everywhere she goes people can feel her radiate and she brings joy to everyone without even really having to do anything. I ask her how her children are, and she says they are doing very well, and they are going to be coming to the Essene community within the year to begin their training. Right now, they are having to be discreetly held.

M: How many children did she have?

C: Three. Two boys that are older. Not old. Maybe, at this time, twelve and thirteen. And a daughter who is nine. The daughter will continue the energetic lineage. So will the boys but they will end up being masters in the Essene community, and the girl will travel and teach. So, I am very excited that her children will be coming soon, and she is too because she does miss them terribly. She knows she will see them soon.

So, it's a long journey. Discreetly stopping in cities and towns. It tickles me. I love traveling and adventure. It is amazing how many people they know — that we arrive in different towns along the way, and we can immediately make our connection and can have places to stay and have an enjoyable evening or daytime until we travel again. But we generally travel at night so that we can be most discrete.

We finally arrive in Egypt and a big market. So, we travel at night and now it's morning. So, this is a huge market, and we go in to get something to eat and then we're to find our friend there. The market is so beautiful. It's like nothing I have ever seen before. The fabrics. The food comes from all over. It's so exotic and beautiful. I want to stay here. I want to just stay in this city.

We go and find our friend who happens to work and oversee what happens inside of the pyramid — the specific rituals that take place and also ritualistic practices that are more spiritual. So, we meet him. We are at his home where he resides. He gives us all beds and we rest for the day because it has been such a long journey. He will feed us and let us rest for a few days before we explore the pyramids.

M: Does he share his name with you?

C: It starts with an A. Arul? Yes, Arul. And he is such a kind man. He is our age. Jesus and Mary. It seems that we are in our early thirties. I feel like I am thirty-

six, but I don't think so. I think I am younger than that.

He is so kind and he takes us back to the market and shows us all the new and exotic things that have come in. And he says that tomorrow we are going to go into the pyramid, and he is going to show us what he has been receiving.

And so, the next morning, before dawn even, we discreetly go to the pyramid with him, and we go down in. I thought you would just walk into the pyramid, but you don't. You go down, down, down, down, and there's all these different corridors.

We go into a special chamber that has a beautiful marble altar in it, in the middle of the room. It's a table for you to lay on, an altar for you to lay on so you can receive the energy. He asks if Jesus wants to go first, and he says yes. So, he gets up onto this slab and Arul holds his ankles. And he is just standing there holding his ankles, and he says that all of the work will be done automatically because where we're at in the pyramid is directly under the center. So, he says just relax and wait and the energy is going to beam down into him, into his heart, and radiate through his heart.

And so, after a moment of breathing, you can see this bluish light coming down from the center. You can't see it physically, but you can sense that it is there. But you can see it going into his body, and it creates this ruby-red energy that permeates him. At first, it's uncomfortable for him. He curls up slightly onto his side, but Arul grounds him with his energy and says to just lie back and relax.

And he says that this energy is going to allow him to upgrade the energy of others, and we will be able to do so as well. All of a sudden there's a flash...like a camera flash, and Arul has to take Jesus off the table. He looks exhausted.

So, in the early morning, before we were doing this, Arul had said there is a specific astrological configuration where energy is the strongest. So, it may take a few days for us to recover. Jesus is literally just like lying on the ground limp, but he's smiling and nodding his head. So, he's okay. I just think that the energy is so strong and concentrated he's just taking some time before he's alright.

Arul says he needs to get someone else on quickly. Mary goes ahead and goes on. The same thing with her. Arul holds onto her ankles and this beam of light comes down, and she starts to shake. She doesn't keel over with the energy. Her whole body is shaking and convulsing, so it seems to know what everybody needs. So, her session is shorter, but it's just as powerful.

Arul lifts her off the table and places her next to Jesus, who's starting to come back. And then it's my turn. After seeing this, I am a bit nervous. He holds onto my ankles, and I feel like my body starts to spin. My head is in one place, but my body is rotating. My head is the focal point. My body is starting to dial round in a circle like the hands on a clock.

I can sense this essence coming. It's like starting to be a tornado, and then the light hits directly into my heart space and it hurts. Through my whole body, it's painful. It's so strong. All the way down to my bones. It flushes everything out of my body and creates this pure radiance. My body starts to shake. not convulsing like Mary's. Like a vibrational hum, small shaking, and then it goes away.

So, I understand how the others felt because you can't move. So, Arul takes me off the table, puts me down next to Jesus and Mary. They've almost come back online. We just lay there. I am not shaking like on the table, but I am still shaking.

A few minutes go by. We start to come back and feel more grounded. And Arul said that this energy for him opened up the chakras in his hands so brilliantly that he said everything and everyone he touches can feel it, and his energy work is so much more powerful now.

So, we thank him, and he invites us back to the place where he resides so we can rest for the next few days.

Our bodies hurt and our energy bodies are aching, but we feel good just the same. Arul said for him it was three days, but for us, it is four to five days to assimilate the energy. We are just laying around, eating minimal but drinking a lot of tea and water. The water is infused with different flowers that Arul gets from the market, to create a high vibration, to help infuse us with that.

Finally, on the fifth day, we are able to leave Arul's place and just go to the market so we can go out and get some fresh air. And we feel radiant but in such a way that when you're coming upon someone, I have telepathic and visionary talents and skills, but almost you can't look at one person and not but know their entire life and know why they are there and what they need assistance with and know all about them just by connecting with their energy.

It's very interesting, and it's almost a little overwhelming to be at the market. And Mary asked, "What are you experiencing?" And I told her, and she is experiencing the same thing. She said it's almost like instantly you know that person's entire life and what they need.

Sorry, I thought that Jesus came to the market too, but Jesus stayed back with Arul to speak with him.

Mary and I are practicing, so to speak, so we pick the same person and then we report to each other about what we saw and about their life and about what they need right now. And we're exactly experiencing the same thing with each person, so this new ability is fascinating. It will be so helpful in healing others and getting to the root of the problem they thought they had but seeing what actually is causing the problem, and so being the most efficient healers we can be.

It's like everything is very bright, almost like looking at life through this white tunnel of light. Almost like we can look upon the Earth in this otherworldly sense. Almost like we are watching ourselves in our human bodies from afar. We are knowledgeably speaking and interacting, but yet we are sitting in the heavens watching — watching it play out like we're watching TV. But we are aware of what we are feeling and what we are experiencing. It's just this connection to Source and divine energy that's really phenomenal because we can toggle our view from that aspect or come into our human body.

M: Makes sense to me. What happens next?

C: We are going to head back. We are going to stay for just a little bit. And Arul says everything that we are experiencing is what he experienced as well. He asked what we thought about bringing people there. We said it's just such a long journey for people to travel there but we would definitely spread the word about it and maybe those that could travel easily would go. And Jesus said he knows that the monks would be interested in coming and their journey would take a very long time but maybe they could stop and stay in the community for a week or so and carry on. He was excited to show them.

He asked Arul if there was a way to take the energy with you or experience that elsewhere, and Arul says that no, it's only in the pyramid, you have to come. And Mary asked what if you replicate a pyramid? And Arul said you may receive the energy, but it would not be in such a heavily concentrated way. We thank him so much for showing the information to us. We are getting ready to depart and we're going to head back to the community.

NEXT SCENE: WORKING WITH THE ESSENE CHILDREN

C: All these kids having fun. They're having fun because we're working with them with the beautiful mystical powers that they have, and they are just elated to be able to put their talents into action. And they're so happy that they're accepted and that there are adults around them to support them, and it makes me happy to see that they can be here — that the world's not so heavy — that they can have fun and they're in a supportive environment. There are all these teachers around them to love them.

M: **Sounds very special. What do you see as you look around? What kind of place are you in?**

C: *I'm in the community — that Essene community. I'm in a courtyard, like an open area; it's not big. So, it's not really a courtyard, but it's an open area. And each child is working individually with teachers on all kinds of different things. So, I'm with one girl, and we're working on the weather and the movement and control of the clouds, and I'm also explaining the proper ways to do that. Where you're not interfering with nature, where it's just helpful if we need a little bit of water or something of that nature.*

M: **How do you discern whether it's helpful or not helpful?**

C: *Just get a feeling from the energies around, just an intuitive feeling that if things are really dry, I can ask if it's appropriate to...if we can have some rain, and then I just can feel. I can feel that's appropriate. So, it's not from a person. It's just from the energy that surrounds us.*

M: **Tell me what is happening as it happens as you let the scene continue.**

C: *I'm working with her, and I asked already earlier in the day if we can work with her about the rain. They said yes. So, I'm showing her how, by sending energy through her gaze in her hands, to manipulate the cloud, and maybe put a few together to condense it smaller so that it'll rain in a specific place. She's able to hover it close to the garden, and then I help her reel it in over the garden. Then we concentrate the energy even more and it rains a little bit on the garden, just as much as we need it and maybe to fill up some vessels that we have there, so we have some water saved.*

There's another boy working with a man, and he's actually creating visible energy between his hands, not a glowing energy, like in electricity, like fibers, like lightning, electricity between his hands. And it's not hurting or burning him, but he's just working with that. And they've got these small boxes, it's like a box with... I'm too far away to see but there's a piece of metal in it and a wire and he can send the actual electricity to this little lamp-type box and then it illuminates. So, from the energy, they have a lamp. Some teachers have these in their places where they stay, their rooms, not many. So, he also wants to work with the boy and tells the boy that part of his duty is to...they're going to learn to build more of these lights so that we can have evening light in that community.

Another woman is working with this little girl on medical, healing ailments, but this is different. She's working specifically through the heart space to then heal the body. We do energy work all the time, but this is a little bit different because it's not science, it's through the heart specifically. She's getting into the person that they're working with, another teacher.

She's focusing her energy so strongly, almost like in a meditation, on the teacher's heart space. The teacher has part of his hand blackened. I'm not familiar with what that is, but she's getting into his heart with her energy healing but also power. There's a power behind that, not just the regular energy healing we do. It's deeper than that and more intensified, and she's able to almost place her essence or her being into his heart to then correct and talk to him about the emotions and what happened that caused his hand to go black. It's almost like she's in a trance when she's doing it, then the black starts to go away and she comes out of the trance. It's almost right before your eyes; it just fades back to flesh. And she comes out of the trance and she's exhausted.

There's one more teacher working with a few kids on telepathy, so he's having them talk to us at random for practice. So, I hear one of them ask me what my favorite color is, so I answer back purple via telepathy. I'm comfortable with it. Some of the other teachers, you can notice, I can see as I look around, that they perk up because they're hearing the question, but they don't feel confident that they can answer back but they just have to think of the answer, and he'll know. The child will know what it is. So, most of the teachers have certain things that are their forte. Some teachers think they can't do everything, but everybody can. It's just a matter of what you're going to work on. Then someone comes out in some robes like we wear and announces that it's time for afternoon meditation, for break, and so we're done with school for the day. Everyone retires back to where they stay. Some people stay in this open area. It's just a free time for everyone to either meditate or pray or whatever they like to do, visit with others before dinner.

M: Let's learn some more. Let's close that scene and move to the next scene that has information. Be there now. Where are you?

C: We're still there but at a different time. There's a big uproar in the community *because the child that works with the electricity accidentally killed another child with it by accident. Now there's a big uproar about using the special powers and the other special talents in the community and a handful of coordinators are trying to figure out what to do there because this is really awful. The healers are trying to work with the child that was affected, but they're not able to bring them back. So, this is very upsetting, and the child is extremely distraught because it was his friend. He didn't mean to do it.*

M: So, this is something you all are able to do, is to bring people back?

C: Sometimes, yes, but in this case, his power was so strong that I don't know that the healers will be able to bring them back.

M: How do people bring souls back? How do they bring people back to life?

C: They just communicate with the soul and ask it to come back to the body. So, if it sees fit, if Council tells it can come back, it can, but if Council says that that lifetime is complete, then it cannot. So, it's not so much we're doing it, we're kind of just helping facilitate its introduction back into the body.

The healers that are most comfortable with the soul retrieval are working with him. The teacher that teaches the boy is one of them. He flags the boy over, so the boy comes over and he's crying and so distraught. And he calms him down and stands up and takes him by the shoulders, and he tells him that he's to help. So, the boy said, no, I can't do that or do anything else. And he said, but you're so powerful that you'll be able to. You're going to be able to do this. We're not powerful enough because he's so young and has this amplified energy.

So, the boy kneels down amongst maybe six or eight people that are surrounding this young boy. When he puts his hands on his heart and his teacher tells him to just lightly pulse the energy within his friend, he's so scared to do it. He says look, he's already...we can't do anything, either that will work or not. So, he pauses first, the teacher, and asks a higher energy that if it is meant for this boy's soul to come back then it will happen now, and then he nods to the boy to pulse the energy. He does and he has his eyes closed and he just freezes there after he pulses the energy. And just like an electric shock through the little boy's body, his eyes shoot open, and he takes a huge gulp of air and sits up. And the little boy just, they both are crying and hugging each other.

The little boy tells the teacher that he doesn't want to do it anymore. And he said, "Oh, no." He said, "Look at what you've done." He's like, this is a miracle. He said, "No, we'll work with it more, so you understand it. It's okay. It's all right." So, everyone is so relieved and just amazed by what just happened. So, they take the boy back to where he stays so he can just kind of rest, but he says really, he doesn't want to rest he's so hungry. So, it's almost time for supper with everyone, so they take them to the eating area. And everybody's milling, talking about the miracle that they just saw. How amazing that happened.

WORKING WITH JESUS AND MARY'S CHILDREN

C: *We're going to release the first group of children. I'll stay in the small abodes, on the mountainside. Then it's time to start with the next wave of children, which is much smaller. In the first wave, maybe there were twenty children, and in this group, there will just be seven. So, Yeshua and Mary's children are there out of the seven. So, they are already comfortable with the abilities that they have, but we're going to dive in because they especially know the little girl has strong, energetic talents that we can dive into more deeply. Yeshua works with her but doesn't have... He wanted someone else to work with her further, to deepen that so that she can connect deeply into their essence and work with them on that level.*

So, we get started. She's very quiet. I'm asking her questions to see what she knows so that we can get started. She says she has a concern. Her concern is what if her essence attaches to another essence and can't let go. So, I tell her about separating. "You're done with your energy work." She was relieved; she didn't know that. She expressed doubts about her abilities. She wasn't sure that she wanted to do this sort of work. I told her let's just explore it and see how you feel when you know a little bit more.

This girl is so powerful. She could gaze upon you, or barely touch your arm, and you could feel the wave of electricity pass through you. It was also an energy straight from the universal life force energy, the Source energy. It was so pure and full of love and compassion. I have never experienced an energy like this before from anyone. It's truly amazing. I'm not going to have one of Yeshua's sons. He's with the raven woman working with telepathy and he's very clear with it so he's going stay with her the entire time. I will work with his oldest son.

He seems like maybe fourteen or fifteen. He's really tall though. We will do energy work as well. So, I'm completed working with his daughter for the day. The son comes over; I think his name is Benjamin. He works in a different way with energy. His is very graceful and is the opposite of his sister's; hers is very powerful and intense. So, I'm working with her on how to control that and make it more smooth. His son already has that ability so that when he engages it's like honey, just very beautiful, golden, warm. Very delicate. So, we work with directing it, so I can tell him more about it, so he has a deeper understanding. We complete our time together. He greatly appreciates the lessons that I've taught him, and he said he's looking forward to coming back tomorrow.

M: So sweet. Did you ever get his other brother's name?

C: Let me see if I can find it? Elijah. His daughter, Seraphina? An absolutely beautiful, little girl.

NEXT SCENE: ANIMAL MAGIC

C: I'm walking down a small corridor to meet with this daughter. And out of her room comes a long serpent — long, thin serpent, like, I don't know, five-feet long. I see her appear in the frame of the room. She's smiling and giggling, and I asked her "What are you doing?" I step aside and the serpent is so beautiful, but it naturally just knows where it's going. She slowly walks behind it and practically escorts it right out. It goes into our side passage and leaves, disappearing into the rocks on the mountainside. I ask her, it is Seraphina, what caused that to happen? Did you bring the serpent in? She's laughing wildly and she said, no, it was in the corner of the room, but she was able to connect with his essence and tell it how to exit safely and it answered back to her. She had never experienced that before. It thanked her because it was frightened and just really wanted to leave back to the mountains.

So, she was laughing and so empowered that she was able to communicate energetically and telepathically with this animal and talk to it as if it was human. Escorting it out as if they were old friends. Yes, so I thought that was amusing as well. I said, well, that's something we'll work on some more then. She's such an exuberant soul. So, we decide to track outside of the community to see if we can find other animals for her to connect with. So, there's a bird. There are not very many animals because it's so dry. They are all in hiding. So, we did find a bird that was looking for water. She could pick it up and I could pick it up as well. So, I said go ahead and instruct the bird how to find the water, which we have water in the inside of our community, which birds can fly over into.

So, she looked at the bird, engaged with it. We both watched as it flew over the wall of our community and came back out, its thirst quenched and very grateful for her assistance. At that, she squealed and laughed wildly again because she was so easily able to connect and talk. So, we end our lesson and Yeshua comes to check and see how she's doing. I tell him about the animals. He says she's always been drawn to them, but she's never communicated with them like this before. So that was wonderful! Then he asks how the meetings in the city are going. I said they're well attended and will continue on even though I'm here training. He said very good. So, then he had expressed that Mary had wanted to talk with me at length and discuss a few things with me. So, I said that would be fine, we can meet, or we can talk at supper. He said that'd be wonderful. So, I say farewell to him and that I'll see him later at dinner.

We seem to have made such a close relationship over the past so many years, so when he talks to me, he almost acts like I'm his sister. Like he will touch the side of my head or hold my shoulder and it's always comforting to see him. He expresses that he's always comforted by my presence as well. So, we head to the area where we eat, and Mary is there waiting, so I go over and sit next to her and ask her what she would like to talk about. She just asked what my experience in the community was growing up, if I enjoyed it. I was away from my parents a lot even though they were in the mountainside close by. I was in intensive training for so long. I said I really enjoyed it and she said she was thinking of traveling on her own, to assist in empowering women more. She would need to leave the children behind, maybe six months, maybe even a year, if I thought they'd be okay with it. I told her yes, there are so many people here that would care and love them.

So, she seemed relieved. I could tell she already had her mind made up to leave. She just needed reassurance that the children would be cared for. She also felt that she was expecting again. She would go on her travels and see what happens. She offered some written tablets, some practices that she does with the women that she would like me to start teaching women that I work with, so I was very open to knowing what that would be. She said it was about how they're teaching in the religious temples about the sacred union. How they're expressing it to be for reproduction purposes only almost, and that's not the case. So, she had practiced for years and still practices with Yeshua, connecting, not running the energy out of your body, and bringing it back into your body, to connect up your spine, to connect with the Source, to connect the circuitry between them.

I thought it sounded wonderful and I could break that out for more women that come and was very intrigued to know where she learned. She said she learned from some of the servants that worked in a monastery in the Far East as they follow that tradition, and they started experimenting with it.

M: When you say the Far East, what would that be in Neomi's modern life?

C: India. Indian mountains. It will take them forever to get there. A long time to travel that far.

M: Thank you. Is this the fourth child that is going to be born from Mary?

C: She believes so.

M: And all of the children are biological and belong to Yeshua?

C: Yes.

M: Wonderful. Tell me what happens next.

C: I assist her in packing and though she's had the other children she's always had midwives help her, so I'm well versed with that. So, I packed her satchels of herbs and things that she may need in the event that her pregnancy comes to fruition. She thanks me immensely and I reassure her that I will continue to work with the children. I will come back to the community and check on them often. I also let her know that if they express that they wanted to stay with me or anything, that I can keep them busy around the palace. They're welcome to do so until she sends for them.

Yeshua comes over and they have such a close connection. They know they can connect (psychically) all the time but there is a sadness in his eyes that he may not see her (physically) for many months. She reassures him it will be just fine. Meanwhile, she expresses that she's so surrounded and encompassed by the Divine that she says that she knows no harm can come to her and laughs, but it's true. It's almost as if she's so divine she can't be touched. So, he knows this but still, they part, and she has all of her things that she needs. I can tell she's holding love for him and sending it to him so as to uplift him because he's just a little sad to see her go. She doesn't want to express her sadness as well. She just wants to express her love. So, she leaves in the evening and Yeshua talks to the children and lets them know that he will be traveling for just a few weeks and then he'll come back and check on them and then we'll see what to do from there.

So, the children are okay with this because they have traveled so much. They enjoy new things and experiencing new places. Seraphina is a little sad to see her parents go, but I reassure her that she can come to the city and stay with me. I will be with them for another few weeks anyway, and she seems comforted by that because we have bonded and have a deep love for each other.

NEXT SCENE: THE FOURTH CHILD

C: So, I am in the kitchen back in the palace. On the edge of the kitchen, there are ornate tables and Seraphina is sitting around, swinging her legs, and she's helping me cut some sort of root vegetable. I have really taken her under my wing. She stays with me. She works on her talents, and she helps me with the meetings with the women. I debated if it was inappropriate for her or not, but it's not. We have been talking about and working with a small group of women about the sacred union. So, we've been practicing that and experiencing such positivity and so much energy and vitality and divine connection. Someone asked me about it and the women come back in and we talk about the experiences and if anyone has anything to share.

Seraphina is extremely curious about this, so she moves closer to the group and slides down the wall. So, we talk, the women and me. The first woman has had great success with it and maybe the emotions that are clarified through you when you're engaging. I ask if anybody had known or figured anything in advance and to share other ways. One of them wants to talk but doesn't. I assure them it's a small group to talk about [this] with so all that's shared is confidential, but she won't come forward. She finally speaks up and she says that the energy rushed up the spine to the skull and she left the body, and was that appropriate, up into the cosmos. And I ask her what alarmed her about that, and she said it was difficult to get back into her body after that. It took her maybe two hours for her to consciously put herself back in her physical body and all along her lungs kept pumping to keep her physical body alive.

M: So, what happens next?

C: One of the people from the community comes by, very urgently and super excited. I am to get my work covered and come back to the community with Seraphina. Seraphina already knows. She knows that her mother came back with a new baby, so she's running. I can barely keep up with her. It's a long trip back. We've already been working all day. And we get back to the community and she runs in, and she embraces her mother and then swoops in to pick up the baby from her mother's arms. She looks to see if she has a brother or a sister. She can't tell, but she wants to figure it out herself. So, I notice she's connecting with the baby to see what kind of energy it has.

She has a puzzled look on her face and her mother says, I know. She can't decipher what the baby is, so she says give it time. She asks what the baby's name is, and Mary says she hasn't decided yet; she just had the baby on the way back and she needs more time to think about it. Seraphina seems a bit disappointed. I say just because the baby doesn't have a name it doesn't mean you can't connect with it. She kind of brings that to her awareness; she is more mindful. She gently helps to take care of her mother, so I let them have their time together. I go and sup with the others and catch up with them. Yeshua is on his way back.

M: Did Mary share where she was traveling when she had the child?

C: *She said she was traveling south, down towards Egypt, towards the pyramids. She wanted more information from the people there about how to move the circuitry of the energy when engaged in the sacred unions so that she can teach it more adequately with others. She found someone who she became very close with that she was able to learn how she needs to engage her energy so that she can explore it more, and she says in time she will practice this with Yeshua so she can be clear in what she is teaching. So, when the baby is a bit older, she will travel back to further her knowledge.*

Yeshua returns and he is elated to see her. Seraphina runs to him. The boys were in the city, and they were called for. Two of the teachers had jobs they could do while they were waiting. He is excited about the baby too. He [told] Mary quietly that he thought the baby was born of two sexes. Mary says that intuitively she thought what happened with the baby, as it got older, it may just be perfect because it blended the masculine and feminine energies — the divine energies together, encompassing that energy in one being, transcending duality. And he is thinking upon this but not yet sure what to make of it, so he spends time with them.

I take Seraphina back to the city, just for a few days until the end of the week. So, she is very excited about going back to the city. She likes it there. As the time has gone by, she seems almost eight. And she asks if she can live with me when her parents travel. I say yes. She expresses her concern about maybe the baby having both sexes. I say we will learn more as the baby gets older. We don't know why it was supposed to be like that. She seems reassured by that.

M: Very good. Let's move forward to the very next scene. The last scene for the day. Be there now. Tell me what you see.

C: *I am back at the community. The whole family is going to travel and depart. They are all going to travel together down towards the pyramids. The man...woman that Mary was apprenticing with has found a small home for them to reside in so that she can continue the training. A few months have passed so Yeshua is interested in moving more with her as meeting with others in Egypt. Seraphina is very sad to leave me, but I reassure her we will see each other often. The children have had the opportunity to fine-tune their abilities and their talents so they can share them with others. So, we all say our farewells and they leave, and they head back to the city. I tell Seraphina to bring me back some beautiful fabric and I can't wait to hear about all of their adventures.*

NEXT SCENE: BASIC TANTRA

C: *Everyone's talking and are excited because...and the kids, his kids, and her kids, that Mary and Jesus are returning from separate journeys. Some of the teachers have been watching their other kids while they left.*

So, Mary arrives first, and she brings the baby. It's much bigger now, maybe eight months old or something. Her kids are so happy to see her; they run up and they've missed each other so much. They just start talking over each other, all the new things they've learned while they've been gone. Then they want to see the baby. So, they're just fawning over their sibling. Then she asks if Jesus has gotten back yet, and she knows he'll return by sunset, so they tell her not yet. She knows he's on his way because he's to meet her there that day. So, she's just so happy to see the kids.

The children all perk up because Jesus has come back, and he came in. So, Mary stands up and they embrace, and then the children start telling their father all the same stories they already told their mother and then when they're done, the children go to eat. A teacher comes to get them and take them. Mary and Jesus start to talk about what she learned in Egypt. It was a fascinating union of energy that you engage with another to combine your energy together so that you can illuminate the energy between the two people so that it is more concentrated and powerful. So, she said, she has learned of these different practices. So, he said that he was fascinated by what she had learned. He had learned a practice where you could leave your body, leave your human body, and you could travel through time with your soul to different places and even leave the Earth and then come back. So, she was very fascinated by this and would like to express wanting to learn how to do that. He said they would probably stay there in the community for probably about a month so that they could rest from their travels and the children could continue to learn. So, he said, after they rest, because they were so weary from traveling for so long, that they'll start to teach each other the practices.

M: Where did Jesus learn these practices? Did he share?

C: From the East, he traveled far east, but very far this time, past the monks he usually works with. I cannot know the name...now was to like China, way past...he doesn't have a name for the teachers. He just calls them teachers. That's how he says the monks.

M: Very good. Let the scene continue to play and tell me what happens next.

C: They decide to go eat with the children. Jesus just wants to be with the baby because he hasn't seen it for so long. And then after they eat everyone's talking to them and asking them about their travels. Then they go to rest and just get the family together and start to rest. But Mary is asking him if he wants to, if she can start to show him some of what she had learned. So, they sit together facing each other. She said we will just start with our telepathy and communicating through our eyes, so that's what they do. They just sit knee to knee, and they just gaze into each other's eyes and start with the telepathy and just talk without talking. They do this for seems like an hour and then she said, that's a perfect start to the practice that they will continue more the next day. He's very fascinated by this practice. He said tomorrow evening because it is most easy to start when you're sleeping at night. He will show her how to leave her body. So, they lie down to rest for the night.

It's the next afternoon, at break time you'd say. The kids are just taking a break. I talk with Mary because she asked how long I'll be there teaching. They said another month before I go back into town to gather the women and teach them some things. She said she wanted to show me the practice that she learned as well so that I can teach the women. So, she asked me to...it's funny because I tell her that I don't know that I'll be able to practice it because I've never been with a man before in my life, even though I'm older. She said that's okay. She said you can do this with a girlfriend or a female friend you have or someone that you're close with. There's some kind of relief because I thought I was going to learn something about something sexual and I wouldn't be able to do it because I was by myself and not really interested so much in that.

So, she has me find my close friend in the community. She and I and my friend and Jesus, we go into where they stay. So, she shows us the gazing. You sit with your partner, just sit in their lap and you keep gazing. Then you can connect by your thoughts, by your energy or touching, whatever that you see fit. Then she explains about starting to run the energy up your spine, through your crown, and into the other person; start to cycle a circle between you. After just breathing and the eye contact and the running of energies, there's this heightened, light-static feeling that runs through you. It just only lasts like a split second. This is almost like a flash of white light, like you're taken somewhere else, just for a split second. She said that's perfect. That's exactly what it is, but then if you practice more, you'll experience that white light and that surge of energy up your spine to your crown for longer periods of time. So, to practice. I asked her what is this for? She says that it helps open your connection to spirit so that you can connect directly and be engulfed in the creative energy, the energy that created us. She said it will open up your mind to many realizations and just inner knowings and wisdom and also remembering.

I personally just feel so elated and energized, just very revitalized, and so does my friend. It's really amazing. So, we agree to engage in the practice every few days so that we can elongate our feeling of connection to that creative energy to see what happens. Mary says as we're practicing, they'll be there about a month too. If I have questions to let her know, so she can guide me to any answers that I need. She would very much like me to teach the other women, the women that come to the spiritual meetings in town so that they can start to engage in the practice with their friends or with their partners.

NEXT SCENE: CRUCIFIXION

C: I can see...I see a...the crucifixion with the other two men. And I'm very saddened by it but I knew, and all of the followers knew, that this was going to be occurring soon, though it's very saddening. I can just see this gigantic, this blinding white, light-blue glow around Jesus and it's so beautiful. It just keeps intensifying and intensifying, then suddenly, you see a blinding flash of light, and the light's gone and his head slumps forward. I know then that his soul has departed back home, but to see this actual light manifest around him, this blinding white light — the edges were beautiful, crystal blue. It was...wow! Very amazing. Then all of us knew, all of his followers knew that it was true — that he went back to Source.

I go back to the temple, and everyone is very saddened by what happened.

We just can't believe that a divine person like that, that he wouldn't find some way to go on because they tortured him so much and so many times. We all knew he was able to heal himself, so he was never...it just didn't dampen his spirit, so we're somewhat dumbfounded why he would choose to go on when he could do so much work. But he has so many teachers and followers now. Maybe he felt that it was his time to move on to the next assignment.

NEXT SCENE: RUMORS OF ASCENSION

C: *My sister and I are working frantically in the kitchen because some of the...someone I work for...so their family came in. So, there are fifteen extra people, so my sister and I are frantically working to cook for them. And one of the other servants comes in and asks if anyone has come to update us on what had happened, and we said, no. And she just kept saying, "He wasn't there. He wasn't there. They didn't find him when his uncle came to get him."*

We all thought maybe he was able to...and Source was able to manifest his body, to just dissipate into dust. So anyway, we were fascinated by it and thought that that was... Wow! Just almost unbelievable. I mean almost unbelievable. We believed it ...but it was just amazing! But it was just a brief talking because, oh, my gosh...just us two having to cook for all these people so we... Hopefully, we'll be able to get together in our women's group and discuss it.

NEXT SCENE: BELIEF IN THE LIGHT

C: *A couple of us ladies were able to get together. There are just three of us. We know the story that the body wasn't there, so we're just talking about different speculations. We mostly all agreed that he just went back to Divine Source and just showed us, really physically, because of the blinding bright, white light with the blue surrounding it...and then the flash and disappearance. There were just so many things that people could see, visibly see, that it was just undeniable.*

How phenomenal, that everyone could actually see what happened and know that that was his soul and energy that left, and we could visibly see it. That was just phenomenal. So, hopefully, we were talking, that it will be easier to spread the word, more, because for something to happen...you couldn't...maybe more people will be interested to see what he had to teach.

EIGHT

Melchizedek, David, Jesus

This session has several timelines giving information regarding the Melchizedek priesthood, the bloodline of David, and events surrounding Jesus's ministry. All these timelines contribute to the incarnation and mission of Jesus as Jesus was said to be a descendant of both Melchizedek and King David via his grandmother Anna the Essene.

C: There are, there's sand beneath my feet. My hands are human. I have sort of a robe on. It seems to be purple with a rope to tie it around the waist. I feel female. I have long flowing dark hair. I'm carrying some sort of pot. There's water or some liquid in it. There seems to be something on the mind. My face and my brows are furrowed. I am in deep thought and thinking about the person I'm going home to.

M: Take me with you on that journey, and it'll get clearer as you walk and journey home.

C: I'm approaching a town. There's still sand on the ground around this town. The walls match the ground, made of dirt or something, dirt or mud. Very square buildings. Looks like a scene out of Aladdin.

M: What makes it look like that? Tell me about it.

C: The style of the houses. The people's dress as they walk by. People don't wave just keep walking.

M: When you arrive in front of your home, tell me what it looks like.

C: It's very small, can see the kitchen immediately when you walk through the door. There's a small, small room that you walk into right away, where you take off your sandals. I see a place to boil water and fire. I see a table in between the kitchen and the entry room. There's a room to the right, closed off by blankets. I move the blankets and go into this room. There's a mat on the floor for sleeping, seems to be a table in the center next to the bed, it's a kind of altar.

M: What kind of things do you have on the altar?

C: Seems some sort of figurine, which I can't make out, a small piece of art.

NEXT SCENE: EATING A MEAL

C: I'm sitting at a table between the kitchen and entry room, and the man is very large, sort of hunched over his food eating ravenously. I'm watching. He must be my partner. It doesn't seem that we're well connected. Like, like we don't understand each other, rather like he doesn't understand who I am or that I understand him.

NEXT SCENE: BAPTIZED BY THE LIGHT

C: I'm standing on the shore of the sea. I'm looking at its vastness, there's sort of a mountain on the bank furthest from me. I'm barefoot. I am appreciating the stillness. There are people here, but I'm away from them. There are some people wading out into the water, about knee deep. We are all wearing white. There's a man guiding people into the water, and he dips them under it in baptism. He puts his hand on their head, on their forehead, says a prayer, dips them down under the water and when they emerge, he gives them a hug. There's a line of people and he's doing this over and over.

M: Will you be receiving it today?

C: It feels like I want to, but I'm not going to. I'm just watching. I'm scared and sad. (crying) I don't know why I won't do it. Everyone looks so happy when they come out.

M: And you just don't feel up to it. What's the sadness about?

C: It has something to do with my partner. He doesn't know what they're doing, he doesn't approve of it. I feel like I'm one of them, but it doesn't look like there are any women going under the water. (Crying) It seems like people have finished being baptized, and they stay there knee-deep in the water, and the man who is dipping who was baptizing them has his arms in the air. (Crying) He seems to be saying something about God. (crying) He's saying the people are clean now. I just continue watching, I want to be clean too. (Crying.)

M: You want to be clean? What feels dirty? What do you want to be cleaned? You can confess it now.

C: (Crying) I don't love my husband. We don't pray properly. (crying) We should pray like the people in the water. (crying) We don't need an altar. (crying) We don't need a figure.

M: You don't need an altar, and they don't need a figure. What do they need?

C: Themselves. I begin walking into the water. (crying) Maybe I can get some approval. (crying) The man giving baptisms has me. His arms are still open. And he puts his palm over my forehead.

M: He puts his palm over your forehead and what happens?

C: He just looks really deep into my eyes, and he doesn't say anything. And then he invites me to dip myself into the water. (crying) I come out of the water even more brightly. They come out of the water. He gives me a huge hug. He whispers something to me I don't understand. I don't know the language. He says that I'm ready. (crying) I feel that I'm ready to be a part of these people like I've always been.

M: Like you've always been what?

C: Part of them. As I move into the group, the faces of disapproval are still there, but they approve more.

M: They're approving of you more now? What happens?

C: The man doing the baptism puts his hands together in prayer over his heart, and I look around, and all the men in the water are doing the same. So, I do it. The sun comes through the clouds over all of us. There is a feeling of purity within myself and in the air.

M: So wonderful, so what will you do next?

C: Feels like I have to go home. I'm exiting the water, turning around, and I see the man who baptized me. He's just watching me, and we hold eye contact for a moment before I turn around and walk home, and there's fear with me as I walk home.

M: What is the fear about?

C: About what I was supposed to do about the man in my house, who does not understand? I come home, he is there at the table where he was eating the night before, but he sees me dressed in white. Like I can't feel how he feels, it's just a look of disbelief.

M: Yeah, so what do you do?

C: I just stand there we're just looking at each other. He doesn't know what to make of my dress and the look on my face which doesn't seem angry with him anymore, which doesn't fear him. Then we're just still looking at each other as if seeing each other for the first time.

NEXT SCENE: MEETING JESUS

C: There is a large gate, with tall walls around it surrounding some other building. People are sort of assembling in front of the gate. I am watching from the outskirts as they gather. I'm unsure what they're there for. The people seem like they are the way I was before I went in the water. They want to but they are scared.

M: So, what happens next?

C: So, I approached the gate and there's somebody sitting on the steps, and people, a small group are gathered around. (crying) He's teaching them. He looks at me as I peek my head in and invites me to come to sit on the steps. There is a small group of people that don't acknowledge me. So, I come closer. The people from outside the gate reject that I should be there.

M: Why is it that you shouldn't be there?

C: It's because I'm a woman. The teacher is not saying anything. He's saying so much. It's so loud, but he's not using any words. I feel the energy growing in my solar plexus. The teacher's arms are spread open embracing all the people sitting on the steps and all the people outside watching. It's like a field of light is surrounding all of us.

M: Describe what this teacher looks like. What does he look like?

C: This one is different from the one who was baptizing people, but the energy is the same. This one doesn't have the same eyes, the one who did the baptism had bright blue eyes. This one is also powerful but is not the same, and the group is different. And he's saying that we can do it. We should do it, to share. Share the light, the light in the presence that we're sitting in is ours, it's everyone's. My hands are now, energy is concentrating in my hands, vibrating, and they feel that they're strong.

M: What else does the teacher say?

C: Our hands are healing hands. We need to go heal the people.

M: Does he share anything else about his guidance for the group?

C: Now, the group is moving away from him now.

M: And what do you do?

C: I never fully joined the group I sort of watched from inside the gate, but on the outskirts of the group. I just stand there looking at him and he's looking at me as if he's feeling me from the steps like he's assessing me. He seems to approve and starts descending from the steps. He's looking at me the whole time, walks right past me, and does not touch me or say anything to me, just walks out the gate, and I'm left there in the courtyard by myself.

M: How do you feel about this exchange?

C: I don't know what to make of it because there's no difference between myself and the teacher. He approved of me, but he did not say anything. I don't know why, but I don't, I don't feel like I need to be part of the group. I don't need to be. I feel like I don't need to learn from him. Feels like I know what I'm supposed to do.

NEXT SCENE: CRUCIFIXION

C: There are two scenes happening at the same time. On one side I can see the place where I was baptized. Now, on the other I can see is the scene of the crucifixion. It feels like it's a foreshadowing, and I'm not actually there. It's like I can see it, but I'm not there, and I'm standing before the lake or the sea, and I can feel this crucifixion occurring before it happens. I understand that things are changing. Big changes are occurring.

M: What's changing there?

C: The world, and the person that, the people who, the people who I'm a part of are facilitating this change, and that the people who are resistant to them, like the soldiers, government, teachers of the law, they're scared.

M: What are they scared of?

C: Scared of this change. They don't want it. They've never wanted it.

M: What's happening there around you? What do you see there?

C: People are kneeling before the cross, it's like there's a phantom of the person on it, but there's not a person really on the cross. People are kneeling before it, and the people who are kneeling before it are chosen. Men who disapproved before welcomed me. First of all, I feel like I'm allowed to be there, and people are so sad. I'm sad too because I understand the great teacher has passed, but I'm not sad like the others because I didn't know him.

M: Tell me more about that.

C: They all were very close with him and learned from him, and I didn't, but I'm still part of them and they don't understand that I understand, but I know that I am, and they know that I am. We're still just kneeling. The energy is very strong.

M: Describe the energy of this place.

C: It's almost as though there is a force field of light all around us. There's a sort of web which forms and arcs out of my crown into the crown of all the other people and we're all interconnected by this sort of light grid between us as we kneel before the cross. This light grid is fueled by, it's blue coming from our crown into the crowd surrounding the cross, being fueled by the yellow golden forcefield energy around the cross, which surrounds us.

M: Tell me what's happening as it happens.

C: Standing up now, seems we're all going our separate ways. As the distance between each of us grows, as we each go our separate ways, the light grid, the blue light grid, which we can access, stays the same, just as strong. Seems like we were in a circle around the cross, and now we're all going in different directions away from it. But despite that, the cross is in us.

M: So where will you go?

C: It's like I'm going south. South, I don't know from where this is. The climate is changing. I'm moving away from the desert. Seeming as if the people are surrounding me like I'm teaching this time.

M: What do you share?

C: There are children and women around me. I am telling them that they have power. That the world is no longer the same place it was, even years ago. I tell them not to be scared and that God is within us, and they all believe me. I tell them that they are the same as me as their husbands don't pray in the same way, but I'm activating these women. I explain to them that they have power. That they are the Earth, they are the earth that they walk on. That the Creator is within them and to know they are creators. In the same way, God brings life, and so do we.

M: And how do they respond?

C: I can see that they want to believe me, but they don't. They don't because of the way of the world, but they want to help me. It seems like some of them do. As they walk away, some of them follow at a distance, and others go home. I continue to walk. I go through more towns, and I continue to do the same thing by myself at all times. I am being followed.

NEXT LIFETIME: MELCHIZEDEK PRIESTESS

C: I'm in a sort of palace. there are long flags hanging down from the wall, which is maybe 30 feet high, a grand entrance, and large steps. I'm walking into the palace. My robes are nice, they're long and they're purple, and I'm walking into this palace as though I belong. I'm walking into a throne room. It feels appropriate to sit on the throne, but I don't do it. I wait.

M: What happens next?

C: A man enters from a room behind the throne, and he has the heir of a warrior.

His furs are over his shoulders, large. This seems to be a different time period from that I was describing previously. There's no throne next to him like there's no queen. This man is light and handsome, very strange looking despite his handsomeness. He doesn't say anything. He just sits on the throne. I'm several steps beneath in my purple gown looking up at him. It seems that I'm giving him counsel. It's occurring to me that I'm telling him about his dreams. I'm explaining to him the steps that must be taken to protect the people.

M: What do you share with him?

C: I'm saying, the plants will wither to trust in God and not man. The living water is within us and water from the sky will not bring the plants to life.

NEXT SCENE: GUIDING THE KING

C: My third center is activated. I'm here in this palace. It seems like people are congregating outside of the palace. The King is watching from the balcony, and the moment I step into his field he feels me. There's a distance between us as we look out at people from the balcony. He seems to have a lot on his mind. The people seem to fully trust this man. He has nothing to say to them and nothing to give them, but he wants to give them everything.

M: So, what do you do?

C: I'm just holding space for him right now. I can feel his doubt growing. He does not, his faith in God is wavering. He wants to have faith, but he doesn't know what it means to be a man, to be mortal. He doesn't understand why he should be placed in charge of all of these people, to be given this false sense of power that he can provide, when only God can provide, and then even still, God is not providing. I am standing near him as he processes this doubt and watches over his people.

NEXT LIFE: MELCHIZEDEK PRIESTHOOD

C: I see some sort of giant turtle. On the side of it, they're giant statues on either side of the turtle. They're guarding the turtle and the turtle is guarding something else. This is very, very old. I can sense multiple priests. They're unlike priests I've ever seen or felt before, and they are aware of my presence. I don't know how many there are. They don't necessarily feel light. They don't feel dark either. They're just powerful.

M: Become aware of your form and tell me what you see.

C: I'm a man. I'm strong with intelligence. Very, very keen set faith in God, the Creator. These men and statues, if they are statues, they seem foreign to me. Like they're from some distant land, but they don't reject me. They don't welcome me. And yet I'm there. As it's like this area's like protected, It's secret and yet I'm there. I can feel these people, but they don't even wonder why I'm there.

M: And why have you come? What is your purpose there?

C: I came to learn. I want to know; I want to know the secrets.

M: What kinds of secrets?

C: About what's really going on on the planet, in this in this ground that we walk because it feels extra-terrestrial. I'm on the Earth, my home, but I know there's more. There are more presences and I need to know.

NEXT SCENE: INNER SANCTUM OF THE PRIESTHOOD

C: I'm in a circular room. It's a dome, but the middle of the dome is open. There are columns around the inside. So, the sun is shining directly through the circle on the top of the dome. It's beautiful. There's grass growing there in the center. Seems to be a kind of altar, and I can't decide if these people are... the term Melchizedek keeps recurring in my head. I can't decide if they are light or not.

M: Tell me what you see and what's happening there in that scene. What do these priests do?

C: It's like they are, it's like I'm in the light and they're all against the closed-off walls, like around the pillars, it's dark. They're sort of in the shadows as I take the scene in, just watching me. I approached the grass in the center, and I sit, and three of them come out in long dark robes. They just look at me. They approve of me. They're willing to teach me, but they don't, I don't know why I came. So, they're unwilling to teach me until I know.

M: So, they've accepted you into this path of learning.

C: Yes, they would not have led me into this space if I was not accepted. It seems as if they were expecting me.

NEXT SCENE: INITIATION

C: There's an altar there in the center now. It seems I'm bringing, being brought to the altar. I'm having visions of being stabbed, but it's as though I'm willing to do this, so I'm not being forced into this ritual. I'm handling it with bravery. I gasp and cry out, but no blood falls. They stab me right in my third center beneath the sternum and blood comes onto the knife, but it doesn't fall from me. A rounded red dagger. They pull it out, there's blood on the end. My skin mends. They place it on the altar.

M: What does this mean there? What happens?

C: I've been given information to carry. Information that I will never forget, like I will always be a student of these priests, but I will never be a priest. It's not who I am. These people are not people. They remain priests throughout their lifetimes. I'm not supposed to be a priest.

M: When you say they're not people, what do you mean by that?

C: They're not from this planet. They may look like they're humans but they're not humans. They know they're not humans. They are here to watch and help humanity. They are the Gatekeepers of Dark and Light, that's why I can't tell if they're dark or light because they're both. This seems to be why they watch humanity because humanity is the same dichotomy.

M: So, these beings, you said Gatekeepers of the Dark and the Light, how does that work?

C: They have rituals. They stand in some sort of circle, perform chants and dances, sort of swaying in a circle which turns into other shapes. The people dance backward and forward, rotating. High, high energies, benevolent energies come. They're welcomed to the center of the circle. They're strange looking. It's not a starship, but just some sort of angelic agent which guides the priests who guide humanity.

M: Is this one being or multiple beings you are speaking of, this agent?

C: It's one thing, but there are many in it. It doesn't have a form. It's showing us some sort of like light form that sort of swirls and moves, but it doesn't need this, it isn't this.

M: So, this energy guides the priests that are upon the Earth?

C: Yes, and the priests guide people whose souls are connected to this agent. These are the indigo children. These are the people whose souls come from other places. This is a light being, and it's assisting the priests and assisting the light beings who are on this Earth. So now, this spirit, a string of light is coming through it, coming away from it and through all the priests. Their hands are together. The light is passing around the circle through all of them. I'm sort of watching this from above. Then, once it's concluded there's like a circle of light and a single beam of light. The Light Being just turned into a huge, it's like lightning from the heavens, and goes all the way up the outer space and then vanishes. It's nighttime, but it's still bright, as the sun is still shining there into the center of the dome.

M: So, what is this light that passes to the priests? What does it do? What's it useful for?

C: This seems to be some information about how humanity will be guided, about how they're to do it. It's about the role that the priesthood will play.

NEXT LIFE: KING DAVID

C: There's a war at the base of the mountain.

M: War at the base of the mountain?

C: People fighting with spears and swords. There's a light at the top of the mountain, and they're so busy fighting that they don't even realize they can both have the light at the top of the mountain. I'm sort of walking through the battle. People are fighting all around me, but I'm just going unnoticed and untouched. Just watching these people. Now, I'm ascending the mountain. I turn around and I see one young man on the outskirts of the battle looking up at the light. He seems to be the only one who understands they all can have it.

M: So, what happens next?

C: The battle is over. There are many dead people there, and the young man who saw the light at the top is part of the side that won. And it seems like people who fought the battle just want to stay at the base of the mountain, they don't want to go up to the light. They're the side won that won the battle.

M: So, what do you do?

C: I'm still watching from the outskirts of the mountain, halfway up the mountain, and just watching and waiting. My eyes are on this young man. Now he's climbing the mountain. He goes to the top and almost as if I'm like a spirit, like no one is recognizing me or ever saw me the whole time he climbed, very strong and handsome. And there's like, it's like a little sun here at the top of the mountain. There's a small plateau, and he sees the light, closes his eyes, and continues walking towards it. Then sits underneath it, just sits, sits, until eventually, the light fills him. In his heart center, and from his heart is a beaming angelic white light, and it's as though angel wings come from around him, huge wings. And it seems that I, I entered this young man, I am him, he is me. He is David. I am clearly human, but I don't look human for some reason. My ears are slightly pointed, my eyes are big, my cheekbones are defined, and still young. Just sitting in this light, I enjoy it. I thank God for helping me to win the battle and helping my people to survive and I for the first time realized that I'm different.

M: How are you different?

C: Others believe in the God in the heavens, and I believe in the God in myself. At the same time, I believe in the God of the heavens.

M: And tell me what happens next.

C: The light which filled me becomes less and less intense to my senses, and I descend the mountain back into the camp. There are men drinking, laughing, eating, and celebrating victory. There's a tent at the end of this camp filled with adornments. It's clearly a regal tent and I enter it, and there is the king in the tent. And I'm realizing for the first time that I'm still a boy, yes, a young man. To the right of this king who, I don't trust him, and he seems to love me and fear me at the same time. Although, I'm just a boy, and to the right of him there's a harp.

M: So, what do you do?

C: I smile at him because I love him, and I go next to him, and he puts his hand on my shoulder, and I begin to play, and the room becomes lighter, becomes lighter.

WORKING WITH HIGHER SELF

HS: He needs to remember who he follows. Where he has learned, who he's been so that he can bring this information into this lifetime. He has strong faith in the power within us all and the memory of the teachings of the priests. He is to lead by example to share with others the truth by his own light. Show them their light within. The priestess had knowledge of the teachings of Melchizedek. She helped the descendants of David remember David's way. He will help to remember forgotten teachings, and he will remind people who, in their past lives, have learned this information.

M: He had said he had some questions about what it means to be from the line of David. What can you share with us about what that means for him?

HS: The house of David is one of the chosen lines, lineages of people who have been divinely guided toward bettering humanity. David was chosen. His DNA was special, therefore, of all the wives that he had, he had so many children, and all of their DNA was special. He is supposed to help activate this DNA in the people who are related.

M: And how can he do this?

HS: Just continue on this path.

Closing Statement

I hope you have enjoyed this journey through the Cosmic Christ Transmissions. I hope that it has inspired deep inquiry and rapid multidimensional healing and awakening, propelling you forward on the path of realizing your own Christhood. Much more is to come as we venture into the NEW EARTH TRANSMISSIONS!

NINE

Family of Light Blessing

Another client named Neli was taken to meet several groups of intelligent beings who are supporting this grand transition.

C: I feel more like a spirit. Like an energy spirit, like a round energy. Yeah, I travel all over. It feels like that. I travel all over if I want to. There are no colors, more transparent. A bright light. Feel safe but still, there is a concern about Earth. Like I am picking up information from Mother Earth. That's the concern. I am receiving information that all is not well. Something has shifted. This energy is coming in, this dark energy. It was not there before. It's like it's moving in from the sky. Like a big storm coming in, but it's not a storm; it's energy. It's dark, and it feels like sticky energy.

NEXT SCENE: JESUS BRINGS THE LIGHT

C: I feel that I am standing on the Earth right now, and I can see all of the rainbow colors. I see Jesus. He's telling me that all is well. That he has come to lift the darkness. And I see him walking the Earth like his footsteps are prints on the Earth. There are some birds flying in the sky. It's showing he takes long walks alone. He can change everything in an instant. It may seem like a long walk, but it can change immediately.

M: When you say it changes, what do you mean?

C: I don't know. I see him dividing the sea. He caught the fish. Miracles.

M: What kind of miracles?

C: Like dividing the fish and dividing the sea and changing the scenery. He's telling us now that we can all do this in this lifetime. We can do this ourselves. That we can welcome this right now, we can welcome change. We have to believe in it. We have to believe that we can. He walked the Earth to show us. He is giving it to us now. It's up to us now.

M: Like he's passing a torch?

C: Yeah. It's time to change gears. It's time.

M: I wonder what he means by it's time to change gears.

C: We have all the answers inside of us. We need to believe it. We need to believe that all is possible; there are so many still going on in our old beliefs. We have new paths to walk now; we have new dimensions to walk. He will walk with us. He wants to walk with us. He has come to do so now with all the humans that are ready to walk with him. He is walking with everyone ready to do so. He's with us. So much, so much. He's here because it's time to take the next step.

M: I wonder what the next step is.

C: It's to act in PURPOSE. To ACT at the next level. To let go of the physicality in the way we believe in it. To understand that everything is energy. It's not what it seems like. The lightworkers are ready now. We have this deep, deep, deep information inside of all of us that is available. It wants to come through us, but we have to go inside. We will never find it on the outside. We find it on the inside out. The deep information it's like soul-level type of information. We have discernment of what we are to give. We have to stay true to ourselves, to our path, to our truth. Nothing but the truth. We all have a flame in our hearts. It has a lot of information; it will show us the way. We need to go inside. When it opens, we go through a new passage. To know ourselves. The grand awakening. We are ready now. We are so ready.

M: How does one go into their heart? How do they unlock it?

C: There are different ways. Every person is to find their way. What makes them feel good. To be romanced. To turn down the volume of the outside and unlock the inside. The best way to do that for yourself is to sit in meditation. For some, it's to take a walk in nature. It takes you into the space where you feel expanded. It's easier now because every step we take, where we are right now, it's going to be easier. I get a picture of the darkness moving into Earth, inside of Earth to the middle part within the Earth; it's also the same picture for us. The darkness has moved further inside.

M: What does that mean?

C: It means it's ready to be released. It needs to be released from the inside, from the inner Light, from the inner realms of Light — where we have lots of lots of lots of Light helping. The darkness can come to light.

M: So, these light beings are helping to clear this dark energy?

C: Yeah, if we turn inward. If we don't turn inward, it will have to play out in the outer.

M: So, the more of us that go inward, the more the energy gets cleared?

C: Wow, yes. It will affect the whole Earth. The whole consciousness of Earth.

M: What happens if we don't go inward. What happens?

C: It will continue to play out the way it used to. We will see a lot of darkness playing out because it's the only way it can be seen. When it's seen, there is a chance for it to transmute into awareness. The faster way is to go inside and ask for the help. I see it's complex; it's like thousands and thousands and thousands of light beings and angels inside. They're just waiting for us to cross over. They're like, "Come on, let's go through this portal so we can receive you, so we can welcome you home." They are so ready to welcome us home. They have waited so long for this.

M: So, this going inward is the way to them?

C: It's the only way.

M: I wonder if they can give us a process of going in so we can connect with them and make the change.

C: It's about being still, not letting your world deceive you or lead you outside to yourself. To practice stillness and to almost see like a lantern inside that grows bigger and bigger. It's like a feeling. The feel of soft alignment. It's not difficult; we are not looking for big things.

SCENE: MESSAGE FROM MARY

C: Mary. I see her. She is so beautiful, giving the divine spark of the divine feminine. She is giving it to us. To humanity. To us all. She is surrounding the Earth with it. She is also in each individual heart. She's holding this soft light like she's showing the way into the heart — the path of softening yourself. To not have expectations. It's like walking through the door, and Mary is on the other side. So close, to be kind to yourself. To be at peace with yourself. To not make life so difficult. To feel like you can always turn inward to the softness because she is waiting there with her soft light taking you through. They are all there taking us through. They are all helping, but Jesus and Mary are coming through because we know them so well.

M: So, because we have more of a collective relationship with them, they are more at the forefront?

C: Yeah. It makes it easier for us.

M: But there is help coming from many?

C: Oh, there are so many.

NEXT SCENE: MESSAGES FROM INNER EARTH

C: Showing a lot of people under the Earth. There are many under the crust of the Earth. They are blue beings. They are here to help us love. They are coming, more and more, to the surface, but we are not quite ready.

M: Do they have anything to share?

C: They will when the time is ready. It's not right now. We need to go through this portal. When we do, they will be available but also help us pass through. It's not time now to be heard. They want us to know they are there.

M: I am wondering, what needs to happen for people to go through this portal? I know many are doing heart-based practices and connecting with their heart. What needs to happen for someone to make the transition?

C: It's on a collective scale. We know about the frustration you must feel that you are working hard to make the passage, but it's more like a tipping point. And it's very, very close to that tipping point right now and that's why we say it has become easier to go inside this portal because when many people do it at the same time, when we practice this all together, it will take over. It will be easier and easier. The tipping point is like being in a new place. Everything will change from the inside out. That's what we are waiting for right now.

M: What are some ways we can accelerate this process?

C: It's this softness. More feminine space. Softness. To allow. Not to run after things, not to try to make it happen, it's more like a process of leaning inwards softly like a soft, warm embrace of ourselves. We don't have to work as much as we used to do. We don't have to work as much on clearing, on clearing our bodies, because it's happening all the time. So, we can drop these exercises more and more and just be. Be the feeling. Be in the center. Take your place in the center of your being. Practice alignment. And then, at the same time, it's a waiting process until the tipping point is reached. The tipping point will happen. It may feel like you are doing too little, but sometimes that is better than doing a lot or doing in general. Everyone can come into a softer focus, and when we allow, things will come to us.

NEXT SCENE: MESSAGES FROM STAR FAMILY

C: (Laughs) Hmm. Oh. I see (laughs) extraterrestrials. They look like small beings, but they have such fun energy. They are stamping and clapping. I see them as a group consciousness.

M: Do they have anything they want to share?

C: They want to share joy! Joy, joy, joy! Lots of joy! They want to lift us into the new with joy. They are sending us the joy — upliftment. It's uplifting energy. Ah, what they are doing — clapping and stamping — they are doing it to raise the vibration. It's actually time to celebrate. It's right around the corner. They are already celebrating. It's so close, and we have come through the darkness, even with what we see play out — it's in the past. It just shows because people are holding it in their perception. It's really in the past.

M: What about when things...I'll give an example that is coming from American culture right now. It's being presented to the whole world how women were hurt in the past and so this is bringing up a strong charge from all the other women who have been hurt by men, by different situations, and I am seeing people grab onto it, attached to that story. How can we individually and collectively work with things like that? That have a charge to it? That have a history of being hurt?

C: It's meant to play out. It's part of the collective. It's part of Earth's memories. Earth is releasing these memories, and of course, every human being is connected to Earth, so it's like an earthquake inside of these human beings. The best way to go about it is to be in love, connectedness, awareness, to embrace and help each other to embrace it. To move in from a high vibration, if possible, to create a high vibration in order to caress it. To envelop it. It needs to be freed; it needs to have its outpouring. It's needed. A deep cry, a deep sense of hurt, it needs to come through, but see it only as the past and not to hang onto it too much. Not have too many stories around it, don't give it too much attention. It's guided to come through.

M: Beautiful. What else are you seeing now?

C: I see the Earth is opening up.

M: What do you see?

C: I see two Earths. And then I see many, many Earths. There are as many Earths as humans. It means that every human has its own individual Earth experience.

M: Beautiful, what happens next?

C: It's the same energy coming through for us; it's the same for us. Our heart energy is the same. The One is returning to us.

M: The same flame in our hearts is in the center of the Earth?

C: Yeah, but also the humans. Every heart is the same material, the same energy, the same One. The same Creator.

M: The energy of the One is in all of us.

C: Yes, and in the center of the Earth as well. In all the Earths. It's time to come together as One.

Closing Statement

I hope that this material has activated multidimensional awakening and expansion for you. I hope that it brings you comfort and joy as we make our way through this transitionary corridor between old Earth and the New Earth. May you count your blessings and walk your path with increasing faith and luminous devotion. The best is yet to come! Much more is to come as we venture into the NEW EARTH TRANSMISSIONS!

ASCENSION LEXICON

I have put together a list of words commonly used in this book and for the topics of awakening, spirituality, and ascension. These are not necessarily defined this way by others but are an excellent way to understand my writings in this book in a more clear and multidimensional way.

-A-

Adamic Form: Original perfected divine human form created for highly developed Light Beings to experience physical creation from within the physical dimension. Fourth Density (4D) body of the New Earth human connecting with oversoul consciousness, higher dimensional beings, and telepathic species.

Agartha: Ancient Inner Earth multi-species civilization with its own sun and ecosystem within the Earth. See *Inner Earth.*

Ain Soph: Kabbalistic term for Source before manifestation into form and translates to "Without Limit" as it is the unlimited creative potential behind all of Creation. Same as "Ineffable" in the Gnostic texts. Can also be written as "Ensof."

Akashic records: Higher-dimensional spiritual records of all experience past, present, and future. Each soul has one. So does each planet and so on.

alchemy: The application of spiritual knowledge to matter to create transformation. This is more commonly known with the Middle Ages' pursuits of turning simple metals into gold. High alchemy being the alchemy of soul/lightbody.

Ancient Egypt: Last golden age of Gaia when many beings held 4th, 5th, and 6th-dimensional consciousness before the descent into lower consciousness (forgetting).

Andromedans: Highly advanced star beings from the Andromeda galaxy assisting humanity's ascension.

Anunnaki: Star beings from the Nibiru system. Sumerian space "gods" who manipulated humanity for personal gain. Now most are in support of humanity's ascension.

apocalypse: 1. Greek word for "unveiling." 2. The dismantling of the mind control matrix and false projections from the controlling forces to reveal to humanity the ugly underbelly and karma of the collective consciousness upon the Earth from this creation cycle which is to be fully reconciled before the planet changes in dimension to Fourth Density New Earth. Not the "end" but a transitionary phase into the next creation cycle.

Archons/Controllers: Term used to describe negatively polarized service-to-self, nonphysical, intelligent beings who siphon negative energy from humanity for their own gain using mind control tactics to keep humanity enslaved through fear and distorted consciousness. The controlling forces behind global institutions. Will be fully dismantled before the shift to New Earth.

Arcturians: Star beings from the constellation of Arcturus assisting Earth with Ascension.

Ascension/ascension: 1. The spiritual maturity process of a soul, moving from an unawakened state of mundane consciousness to multidimensional Source/God-realization described as the movement of the kundalini up the central channel, samadhi, moksha, nirvana, salvation... 2. The movement of Creation into greater states of Glory. 3. The current collective planetary transformation from 3D to 5D consciousness and the New Earth reality.

ascension symptoms: Physical, etheric, mental, and spiritual changes during ascension cycles. Includes headaches, emotional purging, detoxifications symptoms, multidimensional DNA reprogramming, body aches, vivid dreams, and beyond.

Ascended Master: Level of spiritual hierarchy of beings who have ascended in their consciousness enough to no longer need to incarnate in form for spiritual growth but may choose to incarnate to assist the ascension process of a species.

Atman: Divine origin identity, True Self, True Nature, the Witness Consciousness of a lifestream. Same as Brahman. Source Self. Eternally free.

aura: Electromagnetic field of subtle energy that surrounds and pervades the physical body. Contains ever-shifting patterns and geometries of light and vibration that create the template for the physical form.

-B-

biotransducer: organic instrument for transforming energy information for the purpose of manifestation and communication with the universal hologram and divine frequencies. Able to utilize advanced intelligence and spiritual information for the transformation of reality in the human environment.

bodhisattva: Sanskrit term for someone on the path of Buddhahood (ascension) who dedicates their path to the liberation of all beings from cycles of suffering. Able to achieve liberation but delays to assist others in consciousness expansion.

Brahman: The Absolute Reality. Source in impersonal, nonmanifest state. Pure Infinity Existence Consciousness Bliss, *Satchitananda.*

buddhi: the Intellect, reflected consciousness, enlightened consciousness in each person.

buddhic consciousness: enlightened consciousness expressed by *buddhi*, the vehicle for the soul, experienced as profound intuitive insight, unity, and bliss.

-C-

Cabal: Global elite network of negatively polarized service-to-self operatives and organizations working towards complete domination of humanity and planet Earth. See *Archons.*

causal consciousness: the higher mind capacity which utilizes soul memory and intuition to observe and understand manifestation multidimensionally.

centering: Alignment with one's divine nature and inner truth, activating a bridge between Gaia and the Divine through the heart center.

centropy: Regenerative electrification of matter-energy.

chakras: Spiraling transformers of subtle energy with seven primary vortices emanating from the central channel (*sushumna*) which govern our perception of the projected holographic reality and energize our mental and physical processes.

channeling: Opening one's consciousness and vessel as a conduit for subtle energy or other consciousnesses.

Christ: 1. Yeshua ben Joseph (Jesus) in his ascended Lightbody. Forerunner of christ consciousness as part of a divine plan for redemption and restoration of humanity and Earth back to a 4th Density collective. 3. A collective consciousness field that has many emanations and incarnated forms throughout the history of Creation. 4. Title given to one who has achieved consciousness mastery and is "anointed" by Light.

christ consciousness: Also called cosmic consciousness or 5D consciousness. Demonstrated by Jesus of Nazareth in his resurrected 4th Density body.

Christ/Magdalene Lineage: Genetic implantation of higher DNA coding through the offspring of Jesus and Mary. Descendants are worldwide and able to carry a higher light quotient and awaken more easily.

clairaudience: Clear hearing is the ability to hear messages from your Higher Self or spirit beings. This includes hearing the thoughts of other people.

clairgustance: Clear tasting is the ability to receive intuitive information through the sense of taste.

clairesalience: Clear smelling is the ability to intuit information through the sense of smell.

clairvoyance: Clear sight is the ability to perceive information through internal imagery.

clear channeling: Mediumship, or spirit channeling, is the ability to communicate with nonphysical beings and consciousness structures. This can include souls who have passed beyond the veil of physical life or beings that exist in other dimensions.

collective: Representing an entire group, i.e., human collective.

Collective Messiahship: The unification of ascending humanity with the intention of global restoration and ascendency.

cords: Subtle energy attachments that connect us to other beings. Can be negative if developed through limiting beliefs and distorted conditioning.

council: Group of beings joined together with a common focus (i.e., your spiritual council of guides who support your spiritual maturation across lifetimes).

Councils of Light: Groups of advanced spiritual beings that govern the evolution of consciousness and the biological forms of a certain experimental zone to encourage higher states of glory and harmony with the highest being the Universal Council of Light.

-D-

density: 1. Mass per volume. 2. Bandwidth of consciousness reality.

Descension/descension: To go down. The forgetting or falling asleep phases of consciousness. The stepping down of light frequency.

dharma: The noble path of awakening guided through alignment with the Divine through one's True Nature. Exemplified by the life path of beings like Jesus and the Buddha.

The Divine: The frequency emanation that governs and sustains all of Creation across many universes within universes. God Source and the Hosts of Heaven. See *Godhead*.

Divine Androgyny: Harmonic synergy between the divine masculine and divine feminine energetic expressions that results in perfect balance and cohesion.

Divine Creatorship: The birthright of a human to create their life with free-will choice in alignment with their Inner Source.

Divine Feminine: 1. Nurturing creative quality of the Divine 2. Archetypal, spiritual, and psychological ideal of the feminine energetic expression.

Divine Masculine: 1. Administrative quality of the Divine 2. Archetypal, spiritual, and psychological ideal of the masculine energetic expression.

DNA: Genetic blueprint for the development of an organism with both physical and subtle components. Ascended humanity will have 12 fully restored strands.

-E-

Earth Changes: Physical and subtle energetic changes that occur on the planet as it prepares to shift into the next creation cycle. Includes pole shifts, weather changes, seismic and volcanic activity, electromagnetic shifts, and more.

Elohim: First Creation. Creator beings with individual consciousness that work in groups to form Creation. Some created as service-to-all working in unity with Source. Some were created as service-to-self permitted to create in the illusion that they were separate from Source.

empath: Individual who is sensitive to the subtle energy such as thought, and emotional projections of others as they intuitively feel the mental/emotional body of others within their own mental/emotional realm. See *clairsentience.*

End Times: The closing of this current creation cycle where all karma must be balanced, and all shadow revealed so that Earth and spiritually activated humanity can begin the next creation cycle in 4th Density New Earth. See *apocalypse.*

energy: Subtle energy beyond the visible light spectrum ranging from pervasive to neutral to regenerative and life-enhancing. Everything is energy.

energy awareness: Perception of subtle energy in and around one's body.

energy matrix: Geometric organization of subtle frequencies that creates the base structure for the development of form.

entity attachment: Astral debris that has attached itself to a weakened energy system of a host as a source of sustenance and a way to live out "unfinished business." Quite common and easily resolved most of the time by a trained spirit releasement practitioner or energy medicine practitioner.

entropy: Decay and degeneration of matter-energy.

extraterrestrial: From outside of the Earth's biosphere including other planets and universes. There are countless species in our solar system, galaxy, super galaxy, and beyond. Infinite species in infinite realms of creation with many advanced civilizations with histories tracing back trillions of years.

evolution: See *Higher Evolution.*

-F-

false prophets: Teachers and prophets who use spiritual information for service-to-self agendas. Many religious leaders, spiritual teachers, and even those in the ascension community will have their true intentions revealed in the final phases of Ascension.

Family of Light: Physical and nonphysical beings who live their lives in alignment with the Oneness of Creation and the Divine Source. Includes the races of the Star Nations who hold 5D consciousness and higher and the Hierarchy of Light who tend to the many levels of Light Creation.

5D: Consciousness of humans living on the New Earth, can be referred to as christ consciousness or oversoul consciousness.

4D: Awakening stage of ascension bridging mundane consciousness with the New Earth consciousness.

frequency: 1. Rate of vibration measured in hertz (Hz). 2. Higher vibrational rate is likened to positivity and centropy and lower rate towards negativity and entropy.

-G-

Gaia: 1. Sentient Earth 2. Common name for the soul of Earth. Also called Terra.

Galactic Federation of Light: Intergalactic and ultraterrestrial collective of advanced beings who tend to the evolution of consciousness and biological forms throughout the Milky Way. Comprised of advanced scientists, engineers, medical personnel, and other areas of expertise needed to maintain order and balance in the galaxy.

genetic implantation: Seeding of new DNA into the gene pool to evolve a species into higher states of harmony or functionality. Used by the Star Nations and Hierarchy of Light to craft zones of biological experimentation.

gnosis: Direct experience of divine nature through one's own inner being and inner knowing that leads to higher understanding of the nature of the divine reality. See *Knowledge*.

Great Central Sun: Source of all levels of creation in this universe. Brings higher evolutionary coding from Divine Source into other central suns in the universal grid which flow to each solar system evolving each region in accordance with a Divine Plan for Higher Evolution. See *Ishawara*.

Great Divide: The bifurcation of consciousness amongst humanity during the end phases of the planetary ascension process. Includes physical movement across the Earth as humanity moves to be with others of shared consciousness and similar vibration and soul path. Two-world-spit of those who hold negatively polarized, service-to-self consciousness and those of positively polarized, service-to-all consciousness.

Great White Brotherhood: More accurately **Great White Siblinghood**. Ascended Masters, human and non-human, of all gender expressions organized into different orders or councils who tend to the evolution of consciousness and sometimes incarnate to bring new teachings and new energy. Many of these Ascended Masters have aspects of themselves on the planet now to assist the Ascension.

Greys: Extraterrestrial beings from Zeta Reticuli.

God: 1. Supreme Source of Creation 2. Divine Masculine, administrative quality of Godhead, Eternal Mind. See *Ishwara*.

Goddess: 1. Divine Feminine, nurturing, regenerative, creative aspect of the Godhead. 3. Mother God.

Godhead: The Divine Consciousness Source and its various emanations and functions.

Golden Ages: Times of high consciousness and harmony upon the Earth during the Precession of the Equinoxes. (e.g., Avalon, Lemuria)

grounding: The anchoring of one's physical and subtle bodies into the Earth's core through intention, diaphragmatic breathing, and visualization through the Root and Earth Star chakras.

guides: Spiritual beings who assist an incarnated being on their dharmic path towards liberation.

-H-

hara line: Central pillar of light connecting an individual with Gaia and Source.

heart-centered: Action born from inner truth and spiritual ethics through alignment with one's divine nature.

Hierarchy of Light: Various levels of divine consciousness forms, aspects of Source that serve different functions in the evolution of Creation. Ain Soph/Source, Elohim, Archangels, Angelic Realm, Ascended Masters, Ascended Goddesses, Interdimensional Beings, and Restored Humanity in Adamic Form. The Hosts of Heaven.

Higher Evolution: Beyond biological evolution and natural selection, the recoding of experimental zones of the hologram of Creation using divinely encoded frequencies projected through the stellar network which are coordinated by benevolent beings, physical and nonphysical, who serve the evolution of the Divine Plan throughout the Multiverse. Also includes introduction of new genetic expressions into the gene pool, new technologies, and new ideas to be used to evolve the creation into higher order.

Higher Self: 1. The mature part of our consciousness which operates in positively polarized, service-to-all consciousness and is connected to our divine nature. 2. Sovereign self. 3. Harmonic Divine/Human synthesis. 4. Oversoul. 5. Atman.

Holding space: A term used in spiritual growth and self-development circles that means "to hold suffering in an alchemical container of loving awareness so that it may heal."

Holy Spirit Shekinah: The feminine regenerative energy of the Divine. The "presence of God" in the physical dimension. Opening yourself to channel the divine presence begins an alchemical process of light activation that heals and restores all levels of one's being.

-I-

Inner Earth: Ancient and contemporary subterranean civilizations. Many beings went to Inner Earth before the destruction of Lemuria and

Atlantis. See *Agartha*.

intention: Inner resolve to direct one's focus and creative capacity towards a specific goal. *Sankalpa* in Sanskrit.

interdimensional: Existing between dimensions.

intuition: The ability to perceive energy information beyond the five senses before it has become physically manifested in reality. 2. Extrasensory perception.

involution: spiritual consciousness activation that begins as one moves through Ascension and sheds the mind's conditioning.

Ishwara: 1. personal expression of Source. 2. Source in purest manifested form. Commonly called "God" 3. Great Central Sun. 4. Universal Logos.

-J-

Jesus/Yeshua ben Joseph: Master of Light for Earth. Twin flame of Mary Magdalene. Supreme teacher of Divine Love and Ascension. Brought restored DNA and pure Christ Light to the Earth to activate the 4th Density Redemption Plan. Yeshua's cosmic oversoul legacy includes many star systems including the high spiritual schools of Light in the Pleiades and Sirius A and B. His arrival into this dimension of space was the Star of Bethlehem Lightship. His life path was supported by many galactic beings incarnated upon the Earth as well as many extraterrestrials and ultraterrestrial beings. 2. Incarnation of Ascended Master Lord Sananda.

-K-

karma: 1. The sum of a being's actions in this life and in previous existences, both positive and negative actions which influences the soul's path through incarnations.

Knowledge: "Gnosis," divine insight that activates higher consciousness and God-realization. Sanskrit *aparoksha*

kundalini: Serpentine energy originating at the base of the spine that ascends through the sushumna during the awakening process creating ecstatic spiritual expression.

-L-

Lemuria: First advanced human civilization. Often associated with the Pacific Ocean. Destroyed by major flooding and earth changes.

ley lines: Subtle energy pathways that carry evolutionary information across the planetary grid. Also called dragon lines, songlines, telluric lines.

Light: Regenerative divine energy emanations that exist beyond the typical visible light spectrum (Holy Spirit). Different than conventional light from lightbulbs.

Light beings: 1. General term for nonphysical beings of divine origin. See *Family of Light.*

lightbody: 1. subtle body 2. Vital, lower, and higher mind sheaths. 3. Transmigrating soul

Light Conception: The act of conceiving a child directly from the spiritual realms without the need of sperm from a physical being.

Light language: 1. Language spoken through connection to the Divine Presence. Activates multidimensional healing and powerful internal experiences with healing frequencies. Gift of the Holy Spirit, the regenerative creative frequency that quickens and restores all levels of Life. Can be self-initiated or pushed through from the Higher Self and the Divine.

Light Seed: Higher-dimensional, light-encoded genetic material used for Light Conception and altering the genetic composition of a species. Aka *Immaculate Conception.*

Lightship/lightship: Divine craft made by one individual's lightbody/merkaba or a merged merkaba from more than one being for the purpose of interdimensional travel through space-time, stargates, and higher light realms.

Love: Beyond egoic love, unconditional love that is naturally expressed when one develops love for the divine and a service-to-all intention. *Agape* love.

lokas: Sanskrit word for the planes of existence.

loosh: energy of suffering and death harvested by negative human, extraterrestrial, and interdimensional beings which is used to fuel nefarious agendas.

Lyrans: Star beings from the constellation of Lyra. Most commonly known race is the feline beings. First humanoid race in the Milky Way. Original 144,000 oversoul starseeds to bring the human species to Earth.

-M-

magic(k): Use of universal, natural law, and intention to manifest. Can be either service-to-self (dark) or service-to-all (light).

manifestation: The materialization of intention into form.

mantra: Holy names and phrases repeatedly spoken or thought which generate divine thoughtforms to reprogram the physical, etheric, and mental bodies opening one's consciousness to higher perception, divine insight, and union with the Divine. Use of mantra repatterns the DNA, clearing distortion and debris and reprogramming it into higher order and functionality for the projection of divine consciousness light.

Mary Magdalene: Twin Flame and Divine Partner of Jesus. Ancient Egyptian Priestess. High initiate from the Pleiades, Venus, and other high consciousness realms. Arrived at Earth with Yeshua in the Star of Bethlehem Lightship. Gave birth to the offspring of Jesus. This lineage is spread throughout the world.

maya: Illusion. Projecting and veiling power of Source. All that has form and name which tests our ability to see the all-pervasive divine consciousness that supports all manifestations.

meditation: Conscious focusing of the mind on a single object.

merkaba: Divine light vehicle in the auric field that gives one the ability to travel to the higher light realms. Introduced back to humanity through Elijah.

Michael: Archangel who protects and defends all levels of Creation and biological life.

mindfulness: The practice of bringing our life's gross and subtle manifestations into the light of our awareness to observe life in nonduality. Nondual awareness is the ability to see beyond the illusion of duality and see with the eyes of loving awareness.

Mother Mary: Cosmic divine being, a Master soul, who incarnated to give birth to Jesus. High priestess of Ancient Egypt and master teacher of the cosmic priestess arts.

multidimensional: Existing in multiple planes of consciousness, i.e., physical, etheric, mental, and various spiritual dimensions.

Multiverse/multiverse: Universes within universes creating the totality of Creation. What Jesus spoke of when he referred to his "Father's house with many mansions."

-N-

nadis: Pathways of subtle energy in the body. There are said to be 72,0000 that weave in and around the physical body.

New Earth: 1. Higher density light spectrum reality of the ascended Earth. 2. Kingdom of Heaven on Earth.

nirvanic consciousness: liberated consciousness which has transcended suffering, limited egoic identity, and karmic cycles.

-O-

Orion: Constellation with ancient intelligent races with varying levels of consciousness and ranges of polarity. Factions of Reptilian and humanoid beings from Orion fought against Lyrans in the long galactic war.

oversoul: Higher consciousness identity of a soul. Where your individual soul comes from. Collective consciousness of myriad life streams and incarnations. 4th Density/5D Self.

-P-

past life regression: Form of hypnosis or shamanic journeying that evokes information from a client's subconscious mind from previous lifetimes.

Pleiadians: Star beings from the constellation of Pleiades, a highly advanced light consciousness school in our great universe. Cousins of humanity. They implanted upgraded DNA in humanity to open our spiritual connection.

prayer: Approach to the Divine through thought or word which opens the pathways for the living Light to infuse the one who is praying with love and divine insight.

priest: Male devotee of the Divine in service to the illumination of collective consciousness and the ascension of humanity. Administers the will and knowledge of the divine upon the Earth as well as the regenerative, healing presence of the divine feminine.

priestess: Female devotee of the Divine. Often connected to the Goddess. Embodies the wisdom of the divine feminine mothering principle of the Godhead. Matures consciousness in the community into higher states of creativity, sensuality, and grace.

psychic: One who has extrasensory perception. See *intuition.*

pyramids: Sacred architectural sites around the Earth built by various extraterrestrial and ultraterrestrial beings connecting the pathways of vital energy of the Earth with the universal energy grid for the reprogramming of life upon planet Earth. Act as broadcast and receiving systems for information used for planetary evolution.

Prakriti: Manifested reality, transactional reality as opposed to Absolute Reality, maya.

Purusha: Indwelling witness of Creation, Absolute Reality, Brahman, Pure Consciousness. Source Consciousness.

-Q-

quantum: Dealing with the holographic reality and fabric of Consciousness and creation.

quantum consciousness: Holographic consciousness connecting to the matrix of Creation with the ability to focus across time and space through nonlocality and consciousness projection.

quantum healing: Rapid, multidimensional healing that works at the cellular and subtle levels to bring the body's systems into homeostasis. Can be done through psychic processes, shamanic and energy medicine practices, hypnosis, quantum healing technology, star technology, and divine emanations. This is the medicine of New Earth.

quantum mysticism: Emerging evolutionary synthesis between science, metaphysics, and spirituality used to understand Consciousness and the laws that govern Creation.

Qumran: Ancient, multigenerational esoteric Essene community by the Dead Sea in present-day Israel that lived in complete recognition of the Divine through the study and embodiment of divine mystery teachings. Secretive community with advanced star knowledge and superhuman spiritual abilities. Traded knowledge with other global mystery schools and was home and school to Yeshua, Jesus of Nazareth. Yeshua's children studied here as well.

-R-

Reiki: 1. Japanese word meaning spiritual intelligence life force. 2. Intelligently-encoded, divine, redemptive, and regenerative energy from Source. 3. A gift of the Holy Spirit.

Redemption Plan: Cosmic and galactic initiative to restore humanity and Earth back to 4th Density as in the times of Lemuria. Includes genetic implantation, restoration of planetary grid, and operatives incarnating as human to bring new ideas and technologies, broadcasting intelligent and spiritual coding into the biofield of Earth and humanity, and more.

Reptilians: Reptilian humanoid star beings who have had a "negative" influence on Earth who have mostly evolved to positive polarity. Humans have reptilian DNA that gives us our ego mind to assist our perseverance in evolving.

reincarnation: The act of being born again into a new lifestream for the purpose of spiritual growth.

resonance: In spiritual terms, harmonic, synchronous vibrations between two or more objects.

Raphael: Archangel who administers to healing.

-S-

sacred sexuality: Alchemical sexual expression with the intention of uniting with the divine through one's own erotic spiritual nature. Can be practiced alone or with a partner(s).

sacred sites: Holy power spots spread across the planet that form a web of vortex points for subtle energy pathways of the Earth.

samsara: 1. Wheel of Karma 2. rounds and rounds of incarnations on the path of Ascension 3. Suffering mind. 4. Cycles of suffering.

samskaras: Grooves in the mind that create reactive emotions forming our biases, habits, and tendencies. Can be seen as negative or positive.

Self: Divine Self as opposed to the egoic self which is trapped in worldly conditioning.

sentience: The ability to feel, be conscious, or have one's own subjective experience.

service-to-all: Positively polarized, dedicated intention, thought, and action towards the Greater Good and Higher Love as an extension of one's True Self.

service-to-self: Negatively polarized, gives power to false self, ego. Can seem "positive" as intentions can be different than presentation.

sin: Intention, thought, and action that goes against one's inner light that causes an immediate depletion of life force and positive vibration. Serves the egoic self. There is no judgment for this from higher realms. All is for learning and growth. 2. Fear-based judgment system created by religion which connects to belief systems that limit the indwelling of spiritual light by creating perpetual states of fear, shame, and guilt. 3. The fundamental illusion of separation from Source.

Sirians: Star beings from the region of the Sirius A and Sirius B binary star system who have a long, positive history with humanity and are assisting Earth now.

Solaris: Central sun and stargate of our solar system which emanates supraliminal coding for the evolution of the myriad lifeforms in our solar system.

soul: 1. Subtle bodies which transmigrate from one life to the next. See *lightbody.*

spiritual partnership: A relationship that is supported by the desire to assist one another in awakening and healing.

soul contracts: Pre-designed plan and agreements before incarnating for the balancing of karma to propel the path of liberation and ascension. Includes soul agreements between individual souls to play out certain catalyst roles.

soul purpose: Divine intention for a soul for its incarnation encompassing the themes to be explored and lessons to be learned throughout a lifestream. Generally, a soul's purpose is to awaken to Higher Love and Divine Truth.

sovereign: natural consciousness state of the Atman/Self/Inner Source. Human beings embody and reclaim sovereignty through involution and higher consciousness evolution. Able to have agency in all areas of life. Self-regulated. Self-governed.

stargate: Portal used for transportation between long distances and different dimensions.

Star Nations: Space-traveling intelligent species, some positive, some negative, some neutral in relation to humanity and the Earth.

starseeds: Visitors from other schools in the multiverse who have volunteered to live a human life to assist the Ascension of Gaia and humanity. Many of which have experienced ascension mastery in other lifetimes. The best ascension masters from the universe are here on the planet or around the planet in crafts at this time.

substratum: 1. Foundational, base material 2. Source/Brahman/Atman/Pure Consciousness.

superluminal: 1. faster than light

synchronicity: The meeting of two or more seemingly unrelated events or objects that come together in a meaningful way that could even be perceived as divinely coordinated.

-T-

timelines: Pathways of probable events. Infinite potentials and realities fractal out and converge at particular junction points in "time" where choice points exist for the next fractal offshoots of timeline potentials. We are currently moving with multiple timeline potentials for Ascension events that lead to one inevitable event, 4th/5th Density New Earth. Timelines are constantly in flux depending on personal moment-to-moment choices from individuals or the collective meaning the future is never "fixed" but is always in flux. This is the reason why some psychics see different potential probabilities playing out in the future.

3D: Standard human consciousness in its unawakened state, fear/duality-based consciousness which is heavily programmed and hypnotized by the false matrix, the conditioning of the world, and the mind control techniques from the Archons.

Elders: Highest divine council. Progenitors of all cultures in the multiverse.

Twin Flames: Emanations of the same oversoul who assist one another in Ascension. Often uniting at the end of karmic cycles to serve Consciousness. Most commonly thought of as two people in Divine Partnership, but there can be more.

-U-V-W-Y-

Unified Field: The hologram of Creation, the Quantum Field, where all energies and manifestations arise from connecting all through Source Consciousness.

ultraterrestrial: Beings from beyond the physical plane, higher density beings in higher density forms.

vibration: The invisible, subtle layers of matter that form the basic templates for physical reality through repetitive oscillation.

Wisdom: Insight into the Divine Mysteries of Creation and the Godhead that connects us with higher states of divine love and divine grace. See *Knowledge, gnosis.*

walk-in: Exchange of souls during an incarnation. Typically occurs when the original soul consciousness assigned to the body can no longer continue an incarnation from trauma or some other way of vital depletion. A fresh soul consciousness is brought in to accomplish a certain task. Frequently used to bring highly developed galactic beings into the Earth for mission-oriented tasks.

Yeshua ben Joseph: See *Jesus* and *Christ*.

Recommended Reading

The Three Waves of Volunteers and The New Earth by Dolores Cannon
They Walked with Jesus by Dolores Cannon
Jesus and the Essenes by Dolores Cannon
Between Death and Life by Dolores Cannon
Keepers of The Garden by Dolores Cannon
Five Lives Remembered by Dolores Cannon
Return of the Bird Tribes by Ken Carey
Anna: Grandmother of Jesus by Claire Heartsong
Light on Life by B.K.S. Iyengar
The Yoga Sutras of Patanjali (many translations available)
Living Buddha, Living Christ by Thich Nhat Hahn
Reconciliation: Healing the Inner Child by Thich Nhat Hahn
Peace is Every Step by Thich Nhat Hahn
The Path of Energy by Dr. Synthia Andrews
The Seat of the Soul by Gary Zukav
The Book of Knowing and Worth by Paul Selig
The Diamond in Your Pocket by Gangaji
The Magdalen Manuscript: The Alchemies of Horus & the Sex Magic of Isis by Tom Kenyon and Judi Sion
The Kybalion by Three Initiates
Aparokshanubhuti by Adi Shankara
The Upanishads
The Bhagavad Gita
Drig Drishya Viveka
The Keys of Enoch by J.J. Hurtak
Pistis Sophia translated by J.J. Hurtak
The Secret Doctrine by H.P. Blavatsky
Etheric Double by A.E. Powell
The Causal Body and the Ego by A.E. Powell
Regression: Past-life Therapy for Here and Now by Samuel Sagan
Entity Possession: Freeing the Energy Body of Negative Influences by Samuel Sagan

The Illumination Codex

THE ILLUMINATION CODEX
GATEWAY ONE

Ascension Initiation
Keys for Higher Evolution

Michael Garber

THE ILLUMINATION CODEX
GATEWAY TWO PART ONE

Quantum Origins
Keys for Ancient Cosmology

Michael Garber

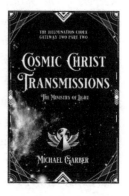

THE ILLUMINATION CODEX
GATEWAY TWO PART TWO

Cosmic Christ Transmissions
The Ministry of Light

Michael Garber

THE ILLUMINATION CODEX
GATEWAY FOUR

Chakra Yoga Discourse
Keys for Higher Consciousness

Michael Garber

THE ILLUMINATION CODEX
GATEWAY TWO PART THREE

New Earth Transmissions
Future Timelines of Gaia

Michael Garber

THE ILLUMINATION CODEX
GATEWAY THREE

Path of Awakening
Keys for Transfiguration

Michael Garber

THE ILLUMINATION CODEX
GATEWAY FIVE

Laying of Hands
Reiki & Beyond

Michael Garber

WWW.NEWEARTHASCENDING.ORG

Support Our Initiatives

Ron and I have dedicated our lives to supporting this Grand Transition. We stand alongside all of you as humanity awakens to its True Nature and becomes a People of Light in the heavenly reality of New Earth.

New Earth Ascending is dedicated to assisting people to realize their divinity and manifest that truth in every aspect of their life. For more information about New Earth Ascending or to contact Michael, please scan the QR code below for a list of resources and links, or visit *www.newearthascending.org*. Be sure to check out our courses including the Illuminated Quantum Healing practitioner course.

New Earth Ascending is a registered 508 (c)(1)(a) Self-Supported Non-profit Church Ministry with a global outreach. We greatly appreciate your support as we create new systems, communities, and schools for the development of the New Earth civilization. If you would like to make a tax-deductible donation to support our mission, please go to:

https://donorbox.org/donationtonewearthascending

Scan with a smart device camera for more information including websites, social media, and more! Bless us all!

Lightning Source UK Ltd.
Milton Keynes UK
UKHW022234041222
413345UK00011B/1393

9 781959 561071